intelligence
A Brief History

Blackwell Brief Histories of Psychology

The *Blackwell Brief Histories of Psychology* offer concise, accessible, and lively accounts of key topics within psychology, such as emotion, intelligence, and stress, that have had a profound effect on psychological and cultural life. The books in this series provide a rich sense of historical context while remaining grounded in contemporary issues and research that will be of interest to both academic and general readers.

Stress: A Brief History
Cary L. Cooper and Philip Dewe

Evolutionary Thought in Psychology: A Brief History
Henry Plotkin

Emotions: A Brief History
Keith Oatley

Intelligence: A Brief History
Anna T. Cianciolo and Robert J. Sternberg

intelligence

A Brief History

ANNA T. CIANCIOLO
ROBERT J. STERNBERG

BLACKWELL PUBLISHING
350 Main Street, Malden, MA 02148-5020, USA
108 Cowley Road, Oxford OX4 1JF, UK
550 Swanston Street, Carlton, Victoria 3053, Australia

First published 2004 by Blackwell Publishing Ltd

Library of Congress Cataloging-in-Publication Data

Cianciolo, Anna T.
Intelligence: a brief history/Anna T. Cianciolo, Robert J. Sternberg—1st ed.
p. cm.—(Blackwell brief histories of psychology)
Includes bibliographical references and index.
ISBN 1-4051-0823-1 (hardcover: alk. paper)—ISBN 1-4051-0824-X (pbk.: alk.
paper)
1. Intellect—History. I. Sternberg, Robert J. II. Title. III. Series.
BF431.C474 2004

153.9'09—dc22

2004005576

A catalogue record for this title is available from the British Library.

Set in 10/12pt Book Antique
by Kolam Information Services Pvt. Ltd, Pondicherry, India
Printed and bound in the United Kingdom
by TJ International Ltd, Padstow, Cornwall

The publisher's policy is to use permanent paper from mills that operate a
sustainable forestry policy, and which has been manufactured from pulp
processed using acid-free and elementary chlorine-free practices. Furthermore,
the publisher ensures that the text paper and cover board used have met
acceptable environmental accreditation standards.

For further information on
Blackwell Publishing, visit our website:
http://www.blackwellpublishing.com

Dedicated to Elena L. Grigorenko,
an inspiration to both of us.

Contents

Figures

Preface

Ideally, science moves in a forward direction. Why, then, should we write a book on intelligence that looks *backward*? A reason that quickly comes to mind is that the history of people trying to understand the basis of intelligent, or adaptive, behavior is interesting. It is replete with controversy and debate, and even has a few shady characters thrown into the mix. It is also littered with brilliant ideas, high hopes, and fascinating discoveries. Moreover, as with other topics in psychology, such as love, conflict and psychopathology, intelligence is a topic of great social interest.

Of course, a great reason for looking back on the history of intelligence is to understand how this history has given rise to the intelligence-testing practices that affect so many people today. That is, it makes good sense to explore the thinking behind different ways of conceptualizing and measuring intelligence because such explorations reveal to us what mental capabilities have been valued in particular times and places and how these values influence the ideas of succeeding generations. Such explorations also lead to challenges of the status quo and eventually to the forward movement critical to science and society. Knowing the current science of intelligence can inform our thinking about today's issues, but knowing the history of intelligence informs the way we should approach tomorrow's challenges.

A final reason to explore the history of intelligence is that knowledge about past failures and mistakes in the exploration of intelligence can help us to avoid the doom of repeating them. Not every approach to understanding intelligence has been enlightened, and some approaches have even retarded the growth of our understanding this complex phenomenon. Because of the tremendous social impact of intelligence research, awareness of the ways that it has been unsuccessful is not just a necessity for enhancing science but is an obligation for improving society.

Our first goal in writing this book is to provide our readers with a basic understanding of the historical trends in the exploration of intelligence and in the application of intelligence research to testing and instruction. Our second goal is to present a balanced history of some of the more controversial topics in intelligence—the genetic and environmental bases of intelligence and group differences in intelligence. We attempt to accomplish these goals by presenting in Chapters One, Two, and Three the multiple angles from which scholars in diverse domains (e.g., psychology, sociology, anthropology, even philosophy) have approached the study of intelligence and by discussing the implications of each approach for measuring and improving intelligence. In Chapters Four and Five, we present the multiple methods and perspectives that have been brought to bear on exploring genes and intelligence and the complex causes for racial/ethnic and sex differences on particular tests of intellectual ability.

Of course, a complete history of intelligence would require several volumes of text, so in the confines of this short book we must make our presentation very brief indeed. Writing a brief history of intelligence requires that we highlight only the most influential theories and practices and that we organize our discussion carefully to share the most information with the fewest number of pages. For this reason, we have chosen not to present this history by listing the signal theories, key findings, and controversial practices in simple chronological order. Instead, we have organized the historical trends in research and application into capsules corresponding to the different ways that psychologists, sociologists, anthropologists, and philosophers have conceptualized intelligence. We believe that presenting the history of intelligence as it followed from different conceptualizations of intelligence highlights how different ways of thinking have influenced the development of intelligence theory and practice.

Throughout history, people have used metaphors to make sense of the complex world in which they live. This practice was exemplified in the popular American film, *Forrest Gump*, where Forrest, a simplistic but thoughtful man, compared life to a box of chocolates in order to characterize life's unpredictability. In Chapter One, we begin our historical review by describing seven metaphors that have been used to conceptualize intelligence and to develop theories for understanding its nature. We highlight the signal theories corresponding to these metaphors, noting that a complete understanding of the complex phenomenon of intelligence requires cooperation among scholars and the integration of multiple ways of thinking.

Once intelligence has been defined, the task of determining how to measure it follows, although sometimes the reverse has been done. For nearly a century, tests of intellectual capability have had a tremendous impact on Western society through their use in diagnosing mental disabilities and in selecting people for educational, occupational, and even military positions. Chapter Two is a presentation of the historical trends in intelligence testing that stem from each of the seven metaphors for conceptualizing intelligence. We first describe assessments developed before rigorous theorizing about intelligence began, and then we describe the testing innovations that followed formal scientific exploration of the nature of intelligence.

Given the tremendous amount of social value placed on intelligence, and its clear role in determining economic success, it is not surprising that people have sought diverse ways to improve it. Some methods for improving intelligence have a more solid scientific basis than others, varying from chemicals believed to enhance neurological functioning to extensive instructional interventions, and each has met with varying degrees of success. We present in Chapter Three the numerous methods used in attempts to improve people's intelligence through instruction. We trace the origins of each method to the metaphors used to conceptualize intelligence, and discuss the overall effectiveness of attempts to enhance intelligence.

In Chapters Four and Five we focus primarily on the research stemming from a small subset of the metaphors used to conceptualize intelligence. This subset of metaphors has a special focus on how people differ in their intelligence and the causes for these differences. It is believed that exploring the causes of intellectual differences among people reveals the mental mechanisms that underlie intelligent behavior. Chapter Four is centered on past and future trends in the exploration of the genetic and environmental bases of intelligence. We describe statistical methods for determining genetic versus environmental influences on intelligence and more modern molecular–genetic methods for understanding how genes influence intelligent behavior. Chapter Five is centered on attempts throughout the history of intelligence testing to determine the complex cause of group differences in intelligence-test scores. We focus primarily on sex differences and racial/ethnic differences, two areas of special interest in the United States.

We conclude our book with a final chapter that looks forward into the future of intelligence. We discuss what we believe to be important directions for future theorizing about the subject, for enhancements in intelligence-test development, for improved intelligence instruction, for deeper understanding of the genetic and environmental bases of intelligence, and for further exploration of the causes of group differences in intelligence-test scores.

This book is intended for interested readers who would like to learn more about intelligence, but who are unfamiliar with the field of intelligence research. It is written to be understandable to learners outside of the academic community, but provides information useful to students completing undergraduate studies in psychology or education. This book also would make a useful supplement for courses in human abilities or the history of psychology taught to advanced college undergraduates. For such purposes, this book will provide broad insight into the key topics of intelligence research and basic issues involved in exploring intelligence, and should be used together with the primary sources referenced within it.

A unique characteristic of this book is that it covers a wide range of topics in intelligence that are typically covered in separate books or are excluded from mainstream presentations of intelligence research because they are scientifically controversial or difficult to communicate. Our coverage allows for the attainment of a basic understanding of the history of intelligence by reading just one book, an understanding that will equip our readers to approach in more depth the main topics of intelligence research in a critical and informed manner. In addition, we attempt to discuss the more socially controversial topics presented in this book in a balanced fashion not typically seen in the mainstream literature. We try to avoid the shrill proclamations made on both sides of a controversy so that we may provide a thoughtful review of the research that has been done so far, how it should and should not be interpreted, and what scientists have yet to learn.

We are grateful to the anonymous reviewer who provided many helpful comments for improving the balance of our presentation of the literature. In addition to achieving balance,

making the translation from entrenched, academic ways of thinking about intelligence to the fresh, but nevertheless discerning,
perspective of the interested learner has been a critical but ardu-
ous process while writing this book. We would like to express
our gratitude to Ms. Heather Ash and thank her for her help in
making our presentation of the topics discussed in this book
accessible and interesting to our readers. We hope they will
gain as much edification from reading the book as we did from
writing it.

Anna T. Cianciolo
Robert J. Sternberg

CHAPTER ONE

The Nature of Intelligence

In the now classic tale, three blind men approached an elephant and were curious about its nature. Having never encountered an elephant before, the men each had a different impression. For the man holding the elephant's thick legs, the elephant was like a tree. The elephant was snakelike to the man who had the elephant's lively trunk in his hands. The third blind man, feeling the elephant's sturdy side, exclaimed it was like a wall.

Who was right? And what does this story have to do with intelligence? Just like the blind men in our story, people exploring the nature of intelligence cannot see the object of their study and so have used metaphors to help them conceptualize intelligent behavior (Sternberg, 1990). In this chapter we describe some of the earliest notions of intelligence, which predate scientific study by hundreds, even thousands, of years. Next we present seven metaphors that underlie modern intelligence research: geographic, computational, biological, epistemological, sociological, anthropological, and systems. We briefly describe each metaphor, highlighting the major theories of intelligence associated with each one.

The first people to ponder the nature of intelligence were not psychologists or educators, but philosophers. The ancient-Greek philosopher Plato likened people's intelligence to blocks of wax, differing in size, hardness, moistness, and purity. A person whose block of wax was overly hard or soft and muddy or impure would suffer intellectual deficits. Thomas Aquinas, writing in the thirteenth century CE, believed the comprehension skills of intelligent people to be more nearly complete and universal than those of unintelligent people. According to Aquinas, however, even the most intelligent person could not approach the omniscience of

God. The eighteenth-century philosopher Immanuel Kant believed that there are different kinds of intelligence or perhaps different facets of intelligence, and that people clearly differed in the degree to which they possessed them.

These (and many other) early philosophical explorations of the human intellect foreshadowed the explosion of intelligence research that would occur in the twentieth century. Even though ideas about the nature of intelligence have existed for thousands of years, much of what we know about intelligence has been discovered since the late nineteenth century. We turn now to the implicit metaphors that appear to have guided scholarly exploration into the nature of intelligence, both historically and in modern times (Sternberg, 1990).

Geographic Metaphor

A map of a geographical region provides us with information about the important features of the region, such as major cities, bodies of water, and political borders. Theories of intelligence that embody the geographic metaphor represent an attempt to develop a map for the human mind. Literal conceptions of "mental maps" can be traced back to the pioneering work of phrenologist Franz-Joseph Gall (see Boring, 1950), who, working in the late eighteenth century, believed that the pattern of bumps and swells on the skull was directly associated with one's pattern of abilities. Although phrenology itself was not a scientifically valid technique, the practice of mental cartography lingered, giving rise to more modern and, one would hope, more creditable theories of intelligence.

More modern geographic theories of intelligence are devoted to identifying the basic intellectual abilities, called ability *factors*, that supposedly underlie the range of intelligent things people can do. The foundation of this approach was the observation that scores on tests of various mental abilities correlated positively with one another, meaning that someone who performed well on one test was likely to perform well on another test and vice versa. Scholars in the early to mid-1900s concluded that some underlying capability (or set of capabilities) must give rise to this relation between test performances, and developed statistical means for identifying basic ability factors. Identifying factors of intelligence is roughly analogous to identifying the health conditions that give rise to a particular set of correlated symptoms (see figure 1.1). An ability factor is analogous to the health condition, and skills measured by ability tests, such as a vocabulary scale or mathematical word problems, are analogous to symptoms. The main differences between the various geographic theories of intelligence are in the number of ability factors (ranging from one factor to 180!) and in the particular factors identified.

One ability factor or many?

Charles Spearman (1927), a British psychologist working at the turn of the twentieth century, proposed two kinds of factors, general ability (which he called "g"), and specific abilities (which he called "s," see figure 1.2). Spearman claimed that g is a single mental capability measured by all intelligence tests, and that it is some form of generalized *mental energy*. Specific abilities are capabilities uniquely measured by a particular mental test, for example, mathematical computation.

Spearman was interested primarily in what is common among various types of intellectual abilities, rather than in what makes each one unique, much as someone wishing to understand the nature of mammals would study what makes seemingly diverse creatures (e.g., mice, humans, dolphins) similar. He believed that specific abilities do not capture the essence of intelligence and instead proposed that important differences in people's mental test scores are due to just one intellectual capability, mental energy. Spearman was not the first person to believe that the human intellect could be described by a single capability, this view can be traced back at least as far as Aristotle (Detterman, 1982). However, Spearman was the first to explore the topic using rigorous empirical and statistical techniques.

Sir Godfrey Thomson (1939), one of Spearman's rivals, proposed that instead of mental energy, g actually consists of many different intellectual capabilities, plus skills and motivation, which operate simultaneously when people take mental tests. As an analogy, the ability to drive a car might appear to be a single skill, but only because multiple skills are all brought to bear on a single larger operation, namely, that of driving the car.

Figure 1.1 Conceptual Representation of Geographic Theories of Intelligence

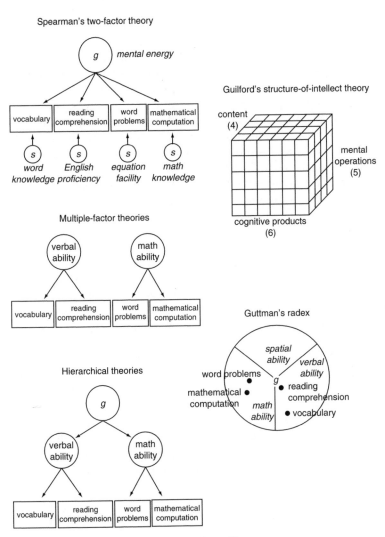

Figure 1.2 *Geographic Theories of Intelligence*

American psychologist Louis L. Thurstone (1938) was perhaps the most influential of the psychologists who disagreed with Spearman. Thurstone contended that intelligence comprises seven distinct but interrelated factors: verbal comprehension, verbal fluency, number (arithmetic computation and problem solving), memory, perceptual speed, inductive reasoning, and spatial visualization. (See figure 1.2 to understand how single-factor theories and multiple-factor theories, such as Thurstone's, differ.) Metaphorically, Spearman proposed one "health condition" underlying a wide set of "symptoms," whereas Thurstone believed there are seven health conditions, each with its own set of symptoms. The idea that there exist multiple intellectual capabilities, and that people can have different patterns of strengths and weaknesses in these abilities, dates at least as far back as the sixteenth century (Detterman, 1982). Like Spearman, however, Thurstone was among the first to mathematically explore the geography of the human intellect (see also Blinkhorn, 1995).

Taking a different approach, J. P. Guilford also argued against the idea of general intelligence, or *g*. His structure-of-intellect theory (Guilford, 1956) involved no less than 120 distinct abilities (see figure 1.2). The abilities in Guilford's theory each involved a different content (figural, symbolic, semantic, or behavioral), cognitive product (units, classes, relations, systems, transformations, or implications), and mental operation (cognition, memory, divergent production, convergent production, or evaluation) aspect. For example, one of these abilities was *memory for semantic units*, measured by a test of word recall. Later revisions of Guilford's theory featured 150, and even up to 180 distinct abilities (e.g., Guilford, 1982). There have been many crippling challenges to Guilford's theory, namely the ubiquitous intercorrelation of ability factors. However, Guilford's work did make an important contribution to test construction in that his content, product, and operation dimensions have proven useful for categorizing types of mental tests.

Hierarchical theories of intelligence – a compromise

In hierarchical theories of intelligence, general intelligence is at the top of the hierarchy, and more specific abilities, such as verbal ability or numerical ability, are lower in the hierarchy (see figure 1.2). Intelligence research at the beginning of the twenty-first century primarily bears the thumbprint of two hierarchical theories, those of John L. Horn and Raymond B. Cattell (1966) and of John B. Carroll (1993).

Horn and Cattell's theory features nine abilities at the top of the hierarchy, but the best known of these abilities are crystallized ability and fluid ability. Fluid ability is defined as flexibility of thought and abstract reasoning capability. Crystallized ability is defined as the accumulation of knowledge and skills. Relatively more recent depictions of ability hierarchies featuring fluid and crystallized ability show fluid intelligence at the top, equated with Spearman's g, and the other abilities below (e.g., Gustafsson, 1984). Carroll's (1993) hierarchical theory, called the three-stratum theory, is based on an extensive reanalysis of nearly every major data set featuring tests of intellectual ability. At the top of the hierarchy (Stratum III) is general intelligence. The second stratum abilities include fluid ability, learning and memory, and perceptual speed, among others. The first stratum, comprising narrow abilities, includes mathematical reasoning (an aspect of fluid ability) and perceptual closure (an aspect of perceptual speed), among others.

Other depictions related to the hierarchical model include the innovative *radex* model, first put forth by Louis Guttman (1954) and later expanded by Marshalek, Lohman, and Snow (1983). In the radex model, ability tests are arrayed along a circle (see figure 1.2). General intelligence is located at the center of the circle. Tests located closer to g measure abilities that are more complex, such as verbal analogical reasoning, and therefore are believed to demand more mental energy. Tests falling closer to the periphery of the circle measure simpler abilities requiring less mental energy, such as short-term memory. Also, tests that are more similar to one another (e.g., vocabulary and reading comprehension) are located closer together in the circle than are tests that are less similar (e.g., reading comprehension and mathematical computation). Phillip L. Ackerman (1988) has extended the radex model to reflect the relative speed requirements of different tests. His depiction of the radex is cylindrical, with tests requiring greater speed in their execution located toward the bottom of the cylinder.

Geographic theories of intelligence have shown us the distinct kinds of abilities that can be measured by mental tests. They also have provided a means for determining how people differ in the degree to which they possess these abilities. However, just as geographic maps do not explain what a river or a mountain range is, geographic theories of intelligence do not explain what an ability factor is. What, for example, is mental energy? Is it the ability to perceive information rapidly? Is it the ability to maintain attention on something in the face of distraction? Or is it something else? Theories based on the computational metaphor have been, in part, an attempt to address this shortcoming, and since the late 1970s theorizing about intelligence has featured various degrees of integration of the geographic and computational perspectives.

Computational Metaphor

Computational theories of intelligence use the computer as a metaphor for explaining what intelligence is. They use terms such as *information processing* to characterize what goes on in the mind when people engage in intellectual activities. One might wonder why it is necessary to explain what intelligence is or how it works. To answer this question, think about an automobile. Just as we know that abilities are required for performing intelligently, we know that engines are required for cars to work. For many of us, this explanation might be all we need; but if we want to go beyond describing our vehicle, for instance to be able to diagnose and fix problems, we would need to know how engines work. Similarly, if we can understand how intelligence works, we can begin to develop ideas for how to diagnose mental disability and improve mental functioning through classroom instruction or cognitive therapy. We will focus our discussion on two types of computational approaches: (1) approaches designed to explain why people differ in their intellectual ability, and (2) approaches designed to understand how intelligence works in all humans.

Origins of the computational approach

Although he is best known for his two-factor theory of intelligence, Spearman (1923) was also one of the first to conceptualize intelligence as a set of cognitive processes. His theory emphasized the importance to intelligent behavior of perceiving stimuli and determining how stimuli are similar and different. The influence of Spearman's work readily can be seen in modern computational theories and was an important beginning for specifying the mental procedures people follow to behave intelligently.

Why do people differ in their intelligence?

Approaches to answering this question have been many and varied, but all have focused on identifying differences in cognitive processes that could explain differences in ability-test scores. In what is called the *cognitive-training* approach (Campione, Brown & Ferrara, 1982), psychologists provide training on a cognitive process they believe to be most important for test performance. If scores improve, they conclude that differences in the efficiency of that cognitive process explain why people have different scores on the test. As an analogy, imagine someone who believes that the most important aspect of baseball pitching is speed. So, he coaches his players to pitch faster balls with the expectation that they will throw more strikes. If they do increase the speed of their pitching but do not throw more strikes, he then concludes that the essence of pitching must not be speed but something else. By exposing the teachability of some cognitive processes, the cognitive-training approach has had some measure of practical relevance. It has not proven viable as a theory-testing approach, however, because it often assumes that all people use the same mental procedures to complete test items, when often they do not.

In the *cognitive-components* approach introduced by Sternberg (1977), intelligence-test problems are broken down into their component parts and the importance of each part to performance on the entire problem is analyzed. For example, if a test problem is the analogy "HORSE is to SADDLE as BIKE is to SEAT," one component involves inferring the relation between HORSE and SADDLE. The components with the strongest and most consistent relation to overall task performance are taken to be the most critical cognitive processes. The cognitive components approach is no longer a dominant approach in modern computational intelligence research, but the influence of this groundbreaking work is evident in current efforts to create test problems that assess particular cognitive processes.

In the *cognitive correlates* approach, introduced by Earl Hunt and his colleagues (Hunt, Frost & Lunneborg, 1973), performance on tasks believed to tap very basic, fundamental cognitive processes (such as retrieving letter names from memory) are correlated with performance on tests of intellectual ability. If the correlation is strong, the basic cognitive process is taken to be critical for test performance. Initial results using this approach were only moderately promising because performance on simple cognitive tasks does not show a strong relation to performance on tests of intellectual ability (Hunt, Frost & Lunneborg, 1973).

The studies of Randall Engle and his colleagues (Engle, Tuholski, Laughlin & Conway, 1999; Hambrick, Kane & Engle, in press) and of Patrick Kyllonen and Raymond Christal (1990) represent more recent applications of the cognitive-correlates approach. This work has explored the relationship between working memory and general intelligence. Working memory is defined as a memory system that has both a storage and a processing component (Baddeley, 1986). It is used when people try simultaneously to hold information in their mind (e.g., a string of three digits) and to execute some kind of cognitive operation on the information (e.g., determining which of the three digits is the smallest). Kyllonen and Christal first demonstrated a strong correlation between working memory and general intelligence. Engle and his colleagues have explored what working memory and general intelligence have in common. They assert that the information processing engaged during working memory tasks involves maintaining attention in the face of distraction, and is an important aspect of all tasks that require working memory or intelligence.

Other investigations of the nature of intelligence also include measures of information processing, such as reacting quickly to a stimulus (Jensen, 1982, in press) and inspecting the similarity/difference of two stimuli (Deary, 1999). In reaction-time tasks, people are asked to respond quickly (e.g., by pressing a button) to the onset of a stimulus (e.g., a light). Jensen found that faster and more consistent responding was associated with higher IQ. In inspection-time tasks, people are given a brief presentation of a pair of stimuli (usually two lines) and must determine if they are the same or different. The amount of time that the stimuli must be shown before a person achieves a certain level of accuracy is called inspection time. Inspection time has shown a notable correlation with IQ and with certain neurological functions (Deary & Caryl, 1997).

How are all people similar in their intelligence?

A subset of computational intelligence research, based in a field of study called cognitive science, has since the 1950s focused on human ability to learn, solve problems, make decisions, and adapt to the environment. For example, one of the computational models developed to explore learning and reasoning processes is based on John Anderson's (1983) ACT* theory of cognition and its more recent extensions (ACT-R, see, for example, Anderson & Schunn, 2000). Anderson has posited that skill acquisition occurs over a series of stages during which people first learn the rules for accomplishing some task, and then create procedures for executing the rules, which eventually become automatic with practice. For example, people learning how to type begin by taking careful note of where they place their fingers. They then learn the patterns of finger movements for creating words and quickly increase the speed with which they execute these patterns. The artificially intelligent computer systems designed by these researchers help us understand how people might learn, apply rules, and use knowledge in order to behave intelligently.

Intelligence research based on the computational metaphor has long held promise for explaining what intelligence is and why people differ in their intellectual abilities. However, human thinking is not computer-like, and the link between the cognitive mechanisms featured in computational theories and actual neurological functions is unclear. Biological approaches to understanding the nature of intelligence provide a means for understanding what exactly happens in the brain during information processing, and how differences in that activity gives rise to differences in intelligent behavior.

Biological Metaphor

Inevitably, when we think about the nature of intelligence, we ponder its origins in the brain. All thought originates in the brain, so eventually we must be able to trace intelligent behavior back to its neurological source. As with computational approaches to understanding intelligence, biological approaches primarily address the questions of (1) why people differ in their intellectual ability and (2) how intelligence works in all humans. Instead of using computational metaphors to answer these questions, the biological approach seeks these answers in the biology of the brain.

For example, to understand why people differ in intellectual ability, the biological approach involves exploring how differences in neurological characteristics, such as brain size or volume, or differences in neurological functioning relate to differences in intelligence-test scores. To understand how intelligence works in all humans, the biological approach involves determining how various intelligent behaviors are represented in the human brain. In short, biological approaches attempt to determine what it is about smart people that makes them "brainy." Research based on the biological metaphor often involves theory and measurement based in the geographic and computational metaphors in order to build a more complete understanding of the nature of intelligence.

Why do people differ in their intelligence?

Numerous techniques for studying the brain and its functioning have been used in the attempt to explain why people differ in their scores on intelligence tests. Dating back to the late 1800s, the measurement of head size (a proxy for brain size) is perhaps the longest-standing and most controversial approach to understanding the cerebral basis of intelligence (e.g., see Gould, 1996). Head size has shown a consistently positive (albeit weak) relationship to scores on various standardized intelligence tests (Vernon, Wickett, Bazana & Stelmack, 2000), indicating that greater head (brain) size is, on average, associated with higher intelligence-test scores. Brain volume has also shown a modest positive correlation with intelligence-test scores (MacLullich, Ferguson, Deary, Seckl, Starr & Wardlaw, 2002; Vernon, Wickett, Bazana & Stelmach, 2000). It is unclear at this time, however, whether brain volume should be considered a cause of greater intelligence or whether factors giving rise to greater intelligence, such as having experienced a larger set of intellectually demanding events, contribute to greater brain volume (e.g., see Garlick, 2002). In any case, the association between brain volume and intelligence appears weak enough to justify searching in other places for the cerebral basis of intelligence.

Technological developments since the late 1800s, such as the *electroencephalogram (EEG), positron emission tomography (PET),* and *functional magnetic resonance imaging (fMRI),* have provided a means for exploring the inside of the working brain in a non-invasive way and for studying the neurological functioning associated with doing particular mental tasks. EEGs record electrical currents in the brain, called *electrocortical activity,* which change as a function of what the brain is doing. PET provides an image of how the brain is using blood flow and glucose while engaged in particular activities. Like PET, fMRI also provides information about what regions of the brain are active during mental tasks, though fMRI uses different techniques and has greater imaging capability. Studies using these technological developments suggest that the efficiency of various neurological functions may play an important role in why people perform differently on tests of intelligence (Vernon, 1993).

Electrocortical Activity

Researchers using an electrophysiological approach to understanding intelligence differences examine the correspondence between intelligence-test scores and the speed of a particular type of electrocortical activity, called P300. The P300 is determined by averaging together several EEGs recorded during the performance of a particular kind of task. P300 occurs in tasks that involve detecting, recognizing, and classifying stimuli. Detecting, recognizing, and classifying are information processes used, for example, when a person recognizes a new brand of orange juice at the grocery store (Vernon, Wickett, Bazana & Stelmack, 2000). Quicker onsets of P300 activity following stimulus presentation typically have been associated with higher intelligence test scores (Deary & Caryl, 1997). This relationship suggests that faster neurological functioning is associated, on average, with greater intelligence. The relation between the speed of P300 onset and intelligence has not been consistent, however, and has been shown to depend on the intelligence test chosen. New developments in electrophysiological approaches involve analyzing how changes in electrocortical activity are related to performance on cognitive tasks (Neubauer & Fink, in press). The results so far indicate that greater efficiency of cortical activity is associated with higher IQ.

Cerebral Blood Flow and Glucose Metabolism

The brain's use of blood and glucose is determined using PET. In PET, a scanner detects photons emitted from a radioactive substance that has been injected into research participants immediately before they perform a mental task. The pattern of photons detected by the PET scanner provides information about how the brain uses blood and glucose during intellectual activities. People performing better on reasoning tasks tend to show less blood flow and glucose uptake while engaged in these tasks (Haier, 2003), suggesting that the brains of more intelligent people are more efficient than those of less intelligent people. This finding is inconsistent across studies, however; higher-ability people have demonstrated *greater* rates of glucose uptake than lower-ability people while performing a relatively difficult task.

Activation Levels

Similar to PET, fMRI also indicates levels of activity in the brain. However, fMRI does not use radioactive substances to trace blood flow. Instead, it uses a very powerful magnet, which generates a magnetic field of nearly 10,000 times the strength of the Earth's natural magnetism. The hydrogen atoms in particular parts of the body align differently with this magnetic field, which allows for relatively precise localization of active brain regions. Information is also provided by fMRI that PET cannot supply about the time course and coordination of neurological activation during the performance of intellectually demanding tasks.

Mirroring findings based on PET, fMRI studies have also indicated that greater levels of activation in the brain are associated with both higher and lower levels of performance (Bunge, Ochsner, Desmond, Glover & Gabrieli, 2001). More specifically, greater levels of activation in certain areas of the frontal lobes have been associated with greater ability to resist interference when performing a working memory task, whereas greater levels of activation in other areas have been associated with lesser ability to deal with working memory load (Bunge, Ochsner, Desmond, Glover & Gabrieli, 2001). In another study, increased activation in areas on the left side of the frontal lobes was associated with concept learning, such that concept learners showed this activation, but nonlearners did not (Seger, Poldrack, Prabha-karan, Zhao, Glover & Gabrieli, 2000).

How is intelligence represented in the human brain?

Scientists use either PET or fMRI to investigate the regions of the brain that "light up" when people engage in intellectual activity. Findings based on the use of PET and fMRI generally support one another (Newman & Just, in press), namely that neurological activity during intellectually demanding tasks is localized in the frontal lobes of the brain (Duncan et al., 2000; see also Engle, Kane & Tuholski, 1999; Neubauer & Fink, in press). The intellec-tually demanding tasks studied have included working memory (e.g., Prabhakaran, Narayanan, Zhao & Gabrieli, 2000) and reasoning (e.g., Christoff & Gabrieli, 2000; Prabhakaran, Rypma & Gabrieli, 2001).

More specifically, the front-most portion of the frontal lobes, called the *frontopolar cortex*, has been implicated in reasoning activities that involve generating and evaluating strategies (Christoff & Gabrieli, 2000). The region of the frontal lobes dir-ectly behind the frontopolar cortex, called the *dorsolateral cortex*, has been implicated in simpler tasks, such as sorting based on color or shape (Christoff & Gabrieli, 2000). In addition, different sides of the frontal lobes have been implicated in doing working-memory tasks that involve spatial and nonspatial processing (Prabhakaran, Narayanan, Zhao & Gabrieli, 2000). Activation in regions on the right side of the frontal lobes has been associated with the integration of verbal and spatial information in working memory, whereas regions on the left side of the frontal lobes have been associated with nonspatial working memory alone (Prabhakaran, Narayanan, Zhao & Gabrieli, 2000).

Although much work remains before the biological approach can provide definitive results about the cerebral basis of intelli-gence, the promise of integrating biological with other ap-proaches for understanding intelligence makes continued efforts highly worthwhile. Indeed, much recent theorizing about intelligence (e.g., Duncan, Seitz, Kolodny et al., 2000; Engle, Kane & Tuholski, 1999; Plomin, 2002) reflects a merging of perspectives based in the geographical, computational, and biological metaphors. With such integrated approaches, we may someday be able to describe precisely how the brain changes as people learn and develop intellectually (see, e.g., Garlick, 2002) and what neurological differences characterize people of different intellectual capabilities.

At this point it is worth to noting that the geographic, computational, and, relatively recently, the biological approaches have dominated much psychological exploration of the nature of intelligence. Much of what we know about intelligence is indebted to work done using approaches based on one or some combination of these perspectives. Perhaps because of the predominance of these perspectives, reviews of intelligence research sometimes exclude other, less traditionally psychological perspectives (e.g., Deary, 2001). We believe that the work of psychologists studying other phenomena (e.g., how intelligent behavior develops), as well as philosophers, sociologists and anthropologists, also sheds light on what it is that allows people to behave intelligently and adapt to the world around them.

In particular, the work of these other scholars suggests ways to systematically characterize intellectual behavior as it occurs outside of the testing situation typically studied by traditional intelligence theorists. This work also suggests ways to begin conceptualizing the role of the environment in the development and expression of intelligent behavior. Ultimately, the findings of this work should inform scientific psychological theories of intelligence because it allows for a more complete representation of what it means to be intelligent. It is therefore necessary to present "alternative" perspectives on the nature of intelligence and to discuss what research based on these perspectives has to offer our understanding of the nature of intelligence.

Epistemological Metaphor

An epistemology is a formal theory of knowledge—its nature, its limits, and its validity. A theory of intelligence that can be called epistemological therefore has knowledge acquisition as its central focus. This kind of theory details how intelligence develops through the construction of a person's thinking processes and knowledge structures. The foundation of epistemological theories of intelligence rests primarily on the work of one psychologist, Jean Piaget, who sought to understand children's acquisition of logical thinking and scientific knowledge. Some readers of this book may already be familiar with Piaget because his profound thinking about mental development has been enormously influential in both the scientific and popular arenas.

Piaget (1972) theorized that intellectual competence develops in a series of four stages, which begin in infancy and are completed by approximately 16 years of age. In the first stage, the *sensorimotor* stage, which spans from birth to approximately two years of age, infants refine and elaborate on innate reflexes, such as grasping and sucking, and begin to discover through trial and error how their actions lead to outcomes. At the end of this stage, children can understand that objects that are out of sight still exist, and can be found if sought.

The second stage, the *preoperational* stage, spans from approximately two to seven years of age. Language acquisition begins during this stage, although thinking about natural phenomena is not yet well developed. Children in this stage display animistic thinking, assigning the characteristics of people or other animals to inanimate objects (e.g., "the fire is hungry for wood").

In the *concrete operations* stage, from the ages of seven through to 11, children can distinguish objects based on their physical characteristics, such as color, size, or shape, and can also order objects, for example, from smallest to largest. The critical cognitive operation acquired during this stage is that of conservation. A child capable of conservation can distinguish between changes in the appearance of a quantity and changes in the quantity itself. For example, such a child knows that she has the same amount of milk whether it is presented in tall, narrow glass or in a short, wide cup.

Children enter the final stage, *formal operations*, around the age of 11 and remain there throughout adulthood. Children and adults capable of formal operational thought exhibit systematic problem-solving skills, including the ability to view a problem from multiple points of view. People in this stage will approach the world in a scientific way, learning by testing their hypotheses about the world and revising their incorrect ideas.

Piaget believed that cognitive development permits children to develop a realistic understanding of the world. In addition to his four stages, he specified two ways that children develop this understanding: *assimilation* and *accommodation* (Piaget, 1972). During assimilation children absorb new information from the environment and fit it into their preexisting knowledge structures. For example, a child would add poodles to his list of dog breeds after seeing one for the first time. To accommodate, children form new knowledge structures to absorb what they have learned. If a child thought that all dogs have long hair, his encounter with a poodle would require him to modify what he believes about dogs.

Neo-Piagetian theorists, including Robbie Case, Kurt Fischer, and Juan Pascual-Leone (Case, 1985, 1999; Fischer, 1980; Mascolo & Fischer, 1998; Pascual-Leone, 1979, 1995), have modified and extended Piaget's original theory. Similar to Piaget's theory, neo-Piagetian theories feature a set of stages or levels of cognitive development, which rely to some degree on physiological maturation. Neo-Piagetian theories also recognize that children play an active role in their own intellectual growth through exploration and inquiry.

Piagetian and neo-Piagetian thinking differ with regard to what develops in each stage and how it is developed. Neo-Piagetian theories often invoke the computational metaphor for explaining how intellectual growth occurs. That is, the development of such information processes as working memory or attention is believed to underlie the acquisition of knowledge and intellectual behavior (e.g., Halford, 1999). Pascual-Leone (1995), for example, believes that a child's progression through the stages of development is a function of the physiological maturation of attentional processes, which allow the child to engage in goal-directed activity and to manipulate greater amounts of knowledge and information at one time. Neo-Piagetians also differ from Piaget in that they embrace the role of environment or culture in shaping the content of people's thought, whereas Piaget did so only minimally (Case, 1999).

Epistemological theories have been critical for turning attention to how intelligent behavior develops, a topic often neglected by theorists guided by the metaphors described previously. However, stage-based theories of intellectual development are problematic because intelligence is fluid in its development and does not exhibit strict, stage-like properties. Sociological accounts of intellectual development may account for the fluid nature of intellectual development, and have arisen, in part, as a response to the limitations of epistemological theories.

Sociological Metaphor

Societal influence on intellectual development is the focus of sociological theories of intelligence. These theories draw attention to the fact that every one of us is a collaborator in the development of people's intelligence. According to these theories, we aid in the intellectual development of others, particularly children, by using language, imagery, and objects to share knowledge and make concepts clearer. We also shape the intellectual behavior of others through our own attitudes about intelligence, intelligence testing, and education.

Like epistemological theories of intelligence, sociological theories of intelligence are founded primarily on the thinking of one psychologist, Lev Vygotsky. Vygotsky (1978) viewed culture as central to intellectual development. He believed that people use what he called *psychological tools* to enhance the thinking of other people. Psychological tools are the language, imagery, thinking styles, and other artifacts in a particular culture used to enhance human mental capability. They work in much the same way that physical tools do to enhance human physical capability.

For example, a more capable cook might aid the thinking of a less capable cook by using language to describe the procedures for making a smooth, flavorful white sauce. The more capable cook would tell her student to be sure to keep the heat under the pan low and to stir the sauce frequently. The more capable cook might also use gestures, demonstrating the sweeping spoon strokes necessary to keep the fluid moving over the heat source. Vygotsky would consider the verbal instruction and the gestures to be psychological tools. Through this instruction, the less capable cook develops his own psychological tools, such as his own set of terminology and procedures for preparing white sauce that he can then pass on to his own students. Language also allows people to regulate their behavior through inner speech, which Vygotsky believed to be critical for learning and intellectual competence.

Vygotsky introduced the concept of the *zone of proximal development* to characterize the situations in which psychological tools are shared and mastered, such as the example of a cook just presented. He defined this zone as the difference between what a person is capable of doing unassisted and what the person can accomplish with help. The greater the difference between what a person can do assisted versus unassisted, the greater the zone of proximal development. *Mediated learning experience*, as defined by Reuven Feuerstein (Feuerstein, 1980), is very similar in spirit to Vygotsky's zone of proximal development. Through mediated learning experience, a more capable person influences the cognitive development of a less capable person by carefully and consciously structuring the learning environment. Feuerstein believed that the instructional effort of the more capable person, or *mediating agent*, was guided by such factors as intention, culture, and emotional investment.

Vygotsky and Feuerstein attempted to identify the processes through which social factors have an effect on cognitive development. More recent work attempts to identify particular societal influences on cognitive development. This work does not typically feature a theory of intelligence, but informs intelligence theory by highlighting the effects that particular socializing agents have on intellectual competence. Such agents include notions of intelligence held in school environments and in family systems.

"School's-eye" views of intelligence

Shirley Brice Heath (Heath, 1983), an ethnographer, studied mismatches between notions of intelligence held in the home and those held in the school environment, and observed the effects of these mismatches on the development of language in children. In three communities, Heath discovered that as home socialization practices diverged from those valued by school environments, performance in school suffered. For example, in one community, verbal interaction typically involved highly fanciful storytelling and clever put-downs. Students from this community experienced difficulty in school, where fanciful stories were perceived as lies, and put-downs were not a valued part of the school's social environment. In another community, parents modeled their verbal exchanges after modes of knowledge transmission in the church, which discouraged dialogue and fantasy. Students from this community excelled in verbatim recall, but experienced great difficulty when novel storytelling was required.

Similarly, Okagaki and Sternberg (1993) found that different ethnic groups in San Jose, California, had rather different conceptions of what it means to be intelligent, which had implications for school performance. For example, Latino parents of schoolchildren tended to emphasize the importance of social-competence skills, whereas Asian parents and Anglo parents tended rather heavily to emphasize the importance of cognitive skills. Teachers, representing the dominant culture, tended to reward those children who were socialized in a view of intelligence that happened to correspond to their own. The rank order of children of various groups according to performance could be perfectly predicted by the extent to which their parents shared the teachers' conception of intelligence.

Family systems

Family systems exert their influence on cognitive development through multiple complex practices, including marital interactions between parents, parenting styles, sibling interactions, and whole-family interactions (see Fiese, 2001). In addition, the way children perceive these practices may also influence cognitive growth. The examination of families has indicated that, in general, parents who are nurturant while maintaining high expectations for intellectual performance tend to have children who exhibit greater levels of intellectual development and school achievement than children whose parents are more permissive (Okagaki, 2001). The positive influence of this parenting style appears to have its effect through increased parent involvement in the child's school activities. The exact mechanisms through which family systems influence cognitive growth are not yet well defined, however, and the effects found are somewhat inconsistent. That is, different parenting styles have different effects depending on the ethnicity of the family, but it is unclear why.

Diverse notions of intelligence generally converge on the fundamental purposes of intelligence — adaptation to the environment and learning from experience. By turning attention to factors outside of the head, sociological views of intellectual development open the door to defining what the environment is for particular people or groups of people, and how environments shape intellectual growth. These views do not, however, shed light on how different environments shape what it means to be intelligent. For insight into this issue, we turn to anthropological approaches for exploring intelligence.

Anthropological Metaphor

Anthropological conceptualizations of intelligence see culture as central to defining what it means to be intelligent. The view that culture is an important influence on the nature of intelligence runs counter to what many believe—that someone who is smart and successful in one culture is largely guaranteed to be smart and successful in another. The concern of anthropologists and many psychologists studying intelligence is that assessments of intelligence can be culturally biased if not designed carefully (Greenfield, 1997). This would result in people being "smart" when they take tests designed by people from their own culture, and "dumb" when they take tests designed by people from other cultures. As shown in Heath's (1983) and Okagaki and Sternberg's (1993) studies above, people in different cultures may develop somewhat different intellectual abilities, depending on what types of intellectual competence are valued by their particular culture.

And, indeed, substantial differences have been demonstrated in conceptualizations of what it means to be intelligent in cultures around the world. Gill and Keats (1980), for example, noted that Australian university students value academic skills and the ability to adapt to new events as critical to behaving intelligently, whereas Malay students value practical skills, as well as speed and creativity. Reviewing Chinese philosophical conceptions of intelligence, Yang and Sternberg (1997) found that the Confucian perspective on intelligence, consistent with the Western perspective, views the intelligent person as spending a great deal of effort in learning, enjoying learning, and enthusiastically persisting in life-long learning. The Taoist tradition, in contrast, emphasizes the importance of humility, freedom from conventional standards of judgment, and full knowledge of oneself as well as of external conditions. Das (1994), also reviewing Eastern notions of intelligence, has suggested that in Buddhist and Hindu philosophies, intelligence involves waking up, noticing, recognizing, understanding, and comprehending, but also includes such things as determination, mental effort, and even feelings and opinions in addition to more cognitive elements.

Studies in Africa provide yet another window on the substantial differences. Ruzgis and Grigorenko (1994) have argued that, in Africa, conceptions of intelligence revolve largely around skills that help to facilitate and maintain harmonious and stable inter-group relations; intra-group relations are probably equally important and at times more important. For example, Serpell (1974, 1982, 1993) found that Chewa adults in Zambia emphasize social responsibilities, cooperativeness, and obedience as important to intelligence; intelligent children are expected to be respectful of adults. Notions of intelligence in many Asian cultures also emphasize the social aspect of intelligence more than does the conventional Western or IQ-based notion (Azuma & Kashiwagi, 1987; Lutz, 1985; Poole, 1985; White, 1985).

It should be noted that neither African nor Asian conceptions of intelligence emphasize exclusively social notions. For example, in a study of Kenyan conceptions of intelligence (Grigorenko, Geissler, Prince, et al., 2001), it was found that there are four distinct terms constituting conceptions of intelligence among rural Kenyans — rieko (knowledge and skills), luoro (respect), winjo (comprehension of how to handle real-life problems), paro (initiative) — with only the first directly referring to knowledge-based skills (including but not limited to the academic).

The examination of cultural differences in how intelligence is defined opens the door not just to creating culturally fair intelligence assessments but also to discovering more universal (as opposed to Western) truths regarding the nature and expression of intelligence.

Anthropological approaches to understanding intelligence arose in contrast to conceptions of culture and mind prevalent in the late nineteenth century. During this period in history, the belief was that cultures, just as the species of all living things, evolved, and that the minds of the members of cultures evolved along with them. The implication of this belief was that more primitive cultures (which were seen as less evolved) were believed to have members with less evolved intellects. Not surprisingly, nineteenth-century Europe was believed to be the pinnacle of cultural and mental evolution, as evidenced by its scientific, technological, and artistic products. The early twentieth-century anthropologist Franz Boas (1911) first challenged the idea of cultural evolution, arguing that the cultural products in different cultures are too different to be comparable.

Revised conceptions of mental evolution followed. These new ideas maintained a strong link between culture and intelligence, emphasizing the importance of the intellect in aiding people to adapt to cultural and ecological demands. The key assertion, however, was that intellectual sophistication must be understood within the context of particular cultural achievements. One important contributor to these ideas was John Berry (1974), who called himself a radical cultural relativist because he believed that cognitive abilities are culture specific and that cross-cultural comparisons of intelligence cannot meaningfully be made.

Berry emphasized the adaptive role of intelligence — that it responds to ecological demands through the development of mental skills that permit successful task performance. For example, he hypothesized that people in a hunting-based culture would have well-developed visual discrimination and spatial skills because the ecological demands of hunting required these skills for successful performance. He ranked several cultural groups according to the importance of hunting to their survival and compared these rankings with test scores for perceptual discrimination and other related skills. He found, as predicted, that people in cultures ranked as having greater dependency on hunting also had higher scores on the psychological tests.

More recently, Berry (2004) has recast his theorizing in less extreme terms. He now acknowledges the existence of universal cognitive processes (e.g., memory, deduction, etc.), but still assigns a critical role to ecology in shaping how intelligence develops in the people of a particular culture. He also maintains what he calls a "value-neutral" conceptualization of cross-cultural differences, meaning that no one culture is seen as more advanced than another.

Adopting a position similar to Berry were Michael Cole and his colleagues at the Laboratory of Comparative Human Cognition (1982). Cole and his colleagues asserted that comparisons of cognitive competence across cultures could be meaningfully made, provided that special care was taken to ensure that tasks used to assess cognitive competence are actually comparable across cultures. For tasks to be comparable across cultures, they must measure the same cognitive capabilities despite surface differences in content. As a very simplistic example, a science test written in English would test science for English speakers, but would largely test guessing ability for non-English speakers. To make the test comparable across the two cultures, a translation, at the very least, would be necessary.

Ype Poortinga and Fons van de Vijver (2004) warn against making assumptions about the nature of cross-cultural differences on tests of intellectual ability. They have demonstrated that carefully designed tests of basic psychological processes, such as memory or reaction time, reveal very little difference in the intellectual capability of people in different cultures. Together with colleague Mustafa F. A. Shebani they found, for example, that memory spans for words in Libyan and Dutch school children were quite different. These differences occurred because Arabic words take longer to pronounce, causing the Libyan children they studied to have slower reading speed. Words that take a longer time to read are more difficult to hold in memory. Memory differences between children in these two cultures were substantially reduced when differences in reading speed were controlled for. Poortinga and van de Vijver recognize that culture often plays a role in test performance, but argue that it is not a foregone conclusion that intellectual competence is different in different cultures.

Anthropological approaches to understanding intelligence raise important questions about ethnocentric influences on experimental and assessment designs. Scientists can unknowingly allow their values to intrude not only into their interpretation of test scores but also into the way they design tests. However, the natural appeal of the anthropological approach can sometimes overshadow the fact that theories of intelligence based on the anthropological metaphor alone are incomplete. They are not intended to address key topics of interest to intelligence theorists, such as why people in the same culture differ in their intellectual capability or how environmental factors influence neurological development.

Systems Metaphor

A system has multiple interdependent parts and its successful overall function is a result of the harmonious interaction of these parts. Computers, national governments, even living things, are all examples of systems. Systems theories of intelligence involve viewing intelligence as a set of multiple interdependent parts, or even multiple intelligences. The successful accomplishment of task objectives or life goals is seen as the result of a complex interaction of these parts. Systems theories of intelligence differ on what these parts are and the nature of their interaction, but all converge on the fact that no single metaphor can adequately describe intelligence. In addition, a key characteristic that distinguishes systems theories of intelligence from other theories that integrate multiple perspectives is that systems theories attempt to address a wider range of intelligent behavior and explicitly posit a role for cultural and other environmental influences on what it means to be intelligent.

Gardner's theory of multiple intelligences

Howard Gardner's (1983, 1999a) theory of multiple intelligences integrates methodological approaches and findings from the geographic metaphor, the biological metaphor, and the anthropological metaphor. Similar to the initial theorizing of geographic intelligence theorists Thurstone and Guilford, Gardner's view of intelligence does not recognize intelligence as a single entity, but rather as a system of independent intelligences. He has proposed eight or possibly more intelligences, which interact to create successful performance, such as in choreographing a Broadway musical or making psychiatric diagnoses. Gardner's intelligences include linguistic intelligence, logical–mathematical intelligence, spatial intelligence, musical/rhythmic intelligence, bodily–kinesthetic intelligence, interpersonal intelligence, intra-personal intelligence, naturalist intelligence, and possibly existential intelligence. Gardner specifies eight prerequisites for the existence of an intelligence, which include biological distinctiveness, unique developmental patterns, and evolutionary plausibility and purpose, among others.

As an example of one intelligence, Gardner defines linguistic intelligence as one's facility with linguistic activity, including reading, writing, listening, and speaking. Professionals, such as journalists, speechwriters, or translators, whose work requires extensive language use, are expected to have a great deal of this intelligence. Gardner uses language disorders produced only by damage to very specific parts of the brain as evidence for the independence of linguistic intelligence from other intelligences. In addition, the evolutionary advantage associated with developing language facility is clear.

Sternberg's triarchic theory of successful intelligence

Robert J. Sternberg's (1988, 1997, 1999) triarchic theory of successful intelligence is an integration of the geographic, computational, and anthropological metaphors. Sternberg defines successful intelligence as the balancing of analytical, creative, and practical abilities to achieve success within a particular sociocultural context. Analytical abilities are used whenever a person analyzes, evaluates, compares, or contrasts pieces of information. Creative abilities are involved in the creation, invention, or discovery of objects or ideas. Practical abilities permit people to practice, apply, or use what has been learned in either formal or informal settings.

Success in life is determined by people's ability to capitalize on their strengths in analytical, creative, and practical abilities and to correct or compensate for their weaknesses. Consider, for instance, a person who has well-developed analytical and practical abilities, but less well-developed creative abilities. In order for this person to be optimally successful, he or she may choose an environment in which analytical and practical abilities are most important for success—perhaps a work team that conducts technical evaluations for outside clients.

The triarchic theory of successful intelligence has three sub-theories, which characterize (1) the mental mechanisms that underlie successful intelligence, (2) the way in which people use these mechanisms to attain an intelligent fit to the environment, and (3) the role of experience in mobilizing cognitive mechanisms to meet environmental demands. Using our example from the preceding paragraph, let us suppose the person conducts a technical evaluation and must decide how to compile and present potentially dissatisfying results to a client. The triarchic theory characterizes the problem-solving process that would be passed through as knowledge gained from previous experience is utilized, strategies created for arriving at a successful solution, the problem solution reached, and new knowledge acquired from the experience.

Sternberg's theory specifies not only the kinds of broad abilities (analytical, creative, and practical) that play a role in achieving success, but also the cognitive processes required to apply these abilities and the problem-solving strategies through which success may be achieved. The theory also recognizes a dynamic aspect of successful performance—that success requires not simply applying acquired knowledge, but also coping with novelty and transforming novel experiences into automatic information processing. It states that successful people find a way to capitalize on their strengths and to correct or compensate for their weaknesses.

Ceci's bioecological model of intelligence

Stephen J. Ceci's (1996) bioecological model involves all of the metaphors of intelligence. Ceci rejected the notion of a single intellectual capability, such as general intelligence, and instead posited multiple *cognitive potentials*, which are biological predispositions that enable particular types of critical thinking and knowledge acquisition. For example, a verbal cognitive potential promotes the acquisition and use of vocabulary and verbal skills. Cognitive potentials, knowledge, and environmental context interact to determine individual differences in the development and performance of intellectual behavior. That is, Ceci claimed that biological endowment is not sufficient for intellectual development, but that such development also requires a supportive environment and motivation to grow.

The knowledge base that people have acquired must also be compatible with the demands of the environmental context. For instance, people may acquire knowledge about how to perform mathematical computations in either educational or informal (e.g., marketplace) settings. People having learned mathematical computation in informal settings have been shown to be facile with math when the calculations involve quantities of familiar objects (e.g., coconuts or other produce) but fail to execute the same calculations when the quantities are presented in an unfamiliar testing situation (Ceci & Roazzi, 1994).

We believe that systems theories represent the future of intelligence research, a future that we hope moves the scientific investigation of intelligence toward a more nearly complete account of intelligent behavior. Rather than each of the other metaphors representing a blind man who only has access to one part of the elephant, the systems metaphor holds promise for revealing the nature of intelligence as a complex whole. However, just as there are countless ways mathematically to arrive at the number 100 (e.g., 98 + 2; 20 × 5), so are there many ways to combine metaphors to understand intelligence. This multiplicity can result in the creation of potentially countless theories, none of which allows us to understand intelligence any better than the others.

Conclusion

In this chapter, we have presented seven metaphors of mind that scientists studying intelligence hold — geographical, computational, biological, epistemological, sociological, anthropological, and systems. We have discussed the major theories derived from each metaphor in order to show how each metaphor has been used to explore the nature of intelligence. Most importantly, we have attempted to demonstrate that a single-metaphor approach to understanding intelligence is limited. Only a combination of multiple metaphors will allow us fully to understand the complex phenomenon that intelligence is and move intelligence research into the future.

The seven metaphors we have described embody the values and interests that intelligence researchers bring to their investigations. Often unknowingly, scientists allow these metaphors to guide the questions they ask about the nature of intelligence and the methods they use to answer these questions. As we discuss in the next chapter, the metaphor one uses for understanding the nature of intelligence has implications for how intelligence is measured.

CHAPTER TWO

The Measurement of Intelligence

Imagine that the three blind men from the beginning of Chapter One decided to measure the "elephantness" of a particular animal. How would each man go about this task? The man who thought that elephants are like trees might measure the diameter of the creature's legs. An animal with thicker legs would be more elephant-like. The man who thought that elephants are snake-like might measure the agility and strength of the animal's trunk or tail. Monkeys with their prehensile tail would be more like an elephant than golden retrievers. The third man, thinking that elephants are like walls, might measure the height and width of the creature. In this case, of course, whales would be more elephant-like than mice.

Just as the three blind men would have created measures of elephantness based on their notion of elephants, scientists design tests of intelligence based on their understanding of its nature. In this chapter, we present a brief history of approaches to mental measurement, focusing primarily on intelligence measurement from the late nineteenth century onward. We also describe several modern intelligence tests, showing how the theory one holds about intelligence influences the tests one uses to measure it.

So, why is intelligence tested, anyway? Psychologists, educators, medical professionals, admissions officers, and employers use intelligence tests to measure differences in intellectual ability between people or to monitor changes in the intellectual ability of a particular person over time. For example, educators use information from intelligence tests to make decisions about who should receive educational assistance or opportunity. Employers or admissions officers may use information about intelligence differences to determine who should be placed in a particular occupational position or school. Medical professionals use intelligence tests to identify mental deficiencies due to developmental deficits, learning disabilities, illness, or head injury. Of course, psychologists use intelligence tests to conduct their research. People of nearly any age, from infants to senior citizens, may undergo a test of intelligence.

Most intelligence tests are similar in many ways to tests of academic accomplishment, such as the SAT, and they are often mistaken for one another. This is in part because the two types of test—intelligence test and achievement test — commonly feature time limits and multiple-choice questions. Moreover, scores from both types of test are thought to reveal important information about a person's mental capability. Finally, both intelligence tests and achievement tests draw, to differing extents, on knowledge acquired in school and sometimes outside it. A key difference between tests of achievement and tests of intelligence, however, is that achievement tests are designed to measure the effects of a systematic program of instruction or training, whereas intelligence tests are designed to measure what a person can do intellectually without the benefit of specific training or education.

Realistically speaking, all tests of mental ability—whether they are intelligence tests or achievement tests—measure both intellectual aptitude and the outcomes of learning. Mental tests fall on a continuum of how specific each test is to particular learning experiences (see figure 2.1). At the most specific, or achievement end of the spectrum, one might find, for example, the final exam

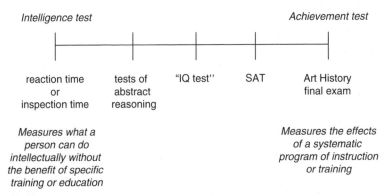

Figure 2.1   *Continuum of Mental Tests*

for a course in art history. At the least specific, or intelligence end of the spectrum, one might find a test of a basic psychological process, such as reaction time or inspection time. But there is no such thing as a "pure" test. Reaction time, for example, may be affected by long-term and even immediate life experiences, such as being fatigued, on the one hand, or having ingested caffeine prior to taking the test, on the other.

One of the earliest known attempts at mental ability testing can be traced back to ancient China, where civil-service examinations were used for hiring government officials. These examinations assessed various skills and abilities, such as archery, horseman-ship, and writing, which were believed to indicate a man's fitness for holding a government office (DuBois, 1970). There have been many other formal (and informal) achievement-testing practices established since these early examinations. In keeping with the theme of our book, our discussion will focus on intelligence testing rather than achievement testing. Intelligence testing began in earnest in the late nineteenth century.

Early Testing

Early attempts to measure intelligence predate the development of formal intelligence theories such as those described in Chapter One. The original intelligence tests we describe below arose from relatively general ideas of what intellectual capability might be, or from practical, rather than scientific, concerns requiring that such capability be measured. For this reason, these original tests are considered pre-theoretical, though they were no less bound to ideas about intelligence than the theory-based tests we will describe in a later section of this chapter. The first intelligence tests were important precursors to the modern, more scientific-ally based intelligence tests we use today, and the more success-ful of these early tests have been modified to measure intelligence as conceptualized by formal theories.

Intelligence as sensitivity

Francis Galton is credited with being the father of mental testing. Galton was a British biologist (and also Charles Darwin's cousin) who believed that the foundation of intelligence rested on one's capacity to exert effort and one's sensitivity to the surrounding environment. In other words, Galton (1883) believed that smarter people have more acute senses (sight, hearing, touch, etc.), notice things more, and, having more information available to them, are better able to compete and succeed. He therefore created several tests of psychological sensitivity, such as one called "weight discrimination." In his weight-discrimination test, examinees were blindfolded, given three identical objects, and were required to arrange the objects in order of increasing weight. A person's sensitivity to weight was determined by the finest difference among the three weights he could discriminate. Interested visitors to Galton's anthropometric (comparative body measurement) laboratory at the South Kensington Museum in London could pay a small fee (three pence) to take this test and similar tests designed to assess other sensitivities.

American psychologist James McKeen Cattell imported Galton's mental-testing practices to the United States. He saw Galton's approach as particularly promising for devising measures of psychological properties that would have the same precision as measures used in the physical sciences (e.g., the Fahrenheit scale for measuring temperature). Cattell (1890) proposed 50 tests, including tests of physical strength, speed of movement, sensory capacities, reaction time, and memory, which when put together would serve as the basis for measuring intellectual capability. Large-scale evaluation of Cattell's tests using college students (Wissler, 1901) did not produce positive results, however. Contrary to expectation, scores on Cattell's tests turned out to be largely unrelated to each other, and to more complex performances requiring intellectual capability, such as college grades. An analogous situation would have been finding that a measure of arm strength was not related to the distance one can throw a javelin. Because throwing a javelin is known to require arm strength, such a finding might call into question whether arm strength was conceptualized and measured appropriately.

Intelligence as judgment skills

French psychologist Alfred Binet's interest in intelligence testing arose from the more practical concern of discriminating between people who could succeed academically and who could not. He and his colleague, Theodore Simon, were part of a commission named by the minister of public instruction in Paris to develop tests that would identify children who did not have the mental capability to benefit from standard educational practices. Children shown via examination to have mental deficiencies were to be placed in special-education programs. Binet and Simon (1916) believed that the foundation of intelligence rested on a set of well-developed judgment skills, and that testing simple psychological processes, such as Galton did, was a waste of time. These judgment skills included being able to direct one's thought to the steps that must be taken to complete a task, to adapt one's strategy during the course of task performance, and to accurately monitor one's performance. To assess these judgment skills, Binet and Simon tested higher level cognitive functioning, such as verbal skills and social comprehension.

Binet and Simon's test was administered to children individually and contained tasks that were arranged in a series of increasing difficulty (Binet & Simon, 1905). Each task was designed to represent the level of performance typical of children at a certain chronological age, ranging from 3 to 13 years. The highest age level at which a child performed successfully was called his or her *mental age*.

Binet and Simon's ideas had greater diagnostic and practical utility than did Galton's and Cattell's. As a result, there have been several revisions of the initial Binet–Simon intelligence test. The first major revision was completed by Lewis Terman (1916). He translated and renamed the test (to the Stanford–Binet Intelligence Scales) for American use, and first used the IQ score, which was introduced by William Stern. Stern defined IQ as the ratio of a person's mental age to his or her chronological age, multiplied by 100. For example, if a six-year-old child performed at a mental age of seven, her IQ would be 7 divided by 6 (1.17) multiplied by 100 (117).

Published 98 years after the original, the 2003 revision, the Stanford–Binet Intelligence Scales, Fifth Edition (Roid, 2003), indicates the staying power of Binet and Simon's nearly century-old ideas. The Stanford–Binet V-is designed for age levels ranging from two to over 90 years and, like the original test, is administered to people individually in an untimed fashion. The 10 tests in the scale together measure reasoning abilities, general knowledge, visual–spatial abilities, and working memory (simultaneous storage and processing of information, see Chapter One). Unlike the original Binet–Simon test, the Stanford–Binet V emphasizes verbal and nonverbal abilities equally. Also, for this scale and all other modern intelligence scales that provide IQ scores, the traditional IQ has been replaced by what is called a *deviation IQ*, which indicates a person's performance relative to other people of the same chronological age.

Practical concerns, this time regarding military recruitment and placement during the First World War, brought about another major shift in early intelligence testing. Tests that could be administered to several people at one time were created in order to meet the United States Army's demands for the rapid testing of a large number of men. The shift from one-on-one testing to group testing required substantial changes to intelligence test design. These changes included (1) the presentation of brief, written items in lieu of more complicated tasks requiring detailed instructions; (2) the replacement of examiner judgment with objective, right/wrong scoring techniques; (3) the imposition of time limits for test completion; and (4) the development of test problems appropriate for adults. The familiarity of these test characteristics to most readers of this book shows how lasting these changes have proven to be.

The staying power of group intelligence tests can be attributed primarily to their tremendous efficiency relative to assessments that must be administered individually. Brief, written items with simple instructions eliminate the need for a highly trained examiner to explain the requirements of each test in the scale. In addition, objective scoring techniques are much quicker and less prone to error than are scoring techniques dependent on the subjective judgment of the examiner. Time limits for test completion have obvious implications for the efficiency of test administration. An important disadvantage to group testing, however, is that it often limits the kinds of performances that can be assessed. For example, basic motor abilities, such as finger tapping or bodily coordination, are not easily assessed when the examinee–examiner ratio is greater than one-to-one.

The Army Alpha, created by Arthur Otis as an adaptation of the Stanford–Binet intelligence scale, was the first group intelligence test developed to meet the Army's recruitment and placement needs during the First World War (see Yerkes, 1921). It assessed various reasoning skills and basic cultural knowledge, and provided a single intelligence score for each examinee. Due to high rates of illiteracy among military recruits, a companion test, the Army Beta, was designed to assess intelligence without requiring knowledge of English. Instead of presenting examinees with written instructions, pictorial instructions were used and examiners pantomimed the requirements of each test. The Army Beta assessed perceptual speed, memory, and reasoning with pictures, and also provided a single score for each participant. Together, the Army Alpha and Army Beta were administered to over a million men, and proved useful for making placement decisions.

Widespread development of civilian group intelligence tests, spearheaded by psychologists involved in the Army test-development work, soon followed. The tests developed at this time included the *Group Test of Mental Ability for Grades 7–12* (Terman, 1920) and the *National Intelligence Tests* (Haggerty, Terman, Thorndike, Whipple & Yerkes, 1923). Tests such as these were used to group students according to ability level and to make decisions about who would be awarded educational opportunities. These tests were precursors to the large-scale achievement testing now pervasive in education.

A major contributor to testing at this time was David Wechsler. Based on his experiences scoring and administering intelligence exams for the Army, he developed his own series of intelligence scales, starting with the Wechsler–Bellevue Intelligence Scale (Wechsler, 1939). This individually administered scale featured both verbal and nonverbal, or *performance*, tests, reflecting Wechsler's belief that intelligence is expressed in both verbal and nonverbal ways. Performance tests require examinees to physically demonstrate their capability at some task, such as completing a drawing or arranging a set of blocks into a particular pattern. Although Wechsler's ideas ran against the common-sense belief that nonverbal, or performance, testing was inefficient, his revised and expanded intelligence scales have been widely used and are still administered today.

Each of the Wechsler scales currently used is designed for a different age group. The Wechsler Preschool and Primary Scale of Intelligence, Version III (WPPSI-III, Wechsler, 2002) is administered to children ranging in age from two-and-a-half years to approximately seven years. Younger children (approximately two-and-a half to four years old) are administered a different part of the scale than are older children. For younger children, the verbal part of the WPPSI-III contains tests of vocabulary and basic knowledge about the world. The performance part of the scale includes tests that require children to create pictures of common objects using jigsaw puzzle pieces and to reproduce a design using building blocks. For older children (approximately four to seven years old) there are additional tests of verbal comprehension and perceptual classification skills. Also, both the verbal and performance parts of the WPPSI-III for older children contain additional tests that assess reasoning. The overall score, or Full-Scale IQ, on the WPPSI-III is slightly different for younger and older children. For younger children, it is composed of a Verbal Comprehension Index (VCI) and a Perceptual Organization Index (POI). For older children, it is composed of a VCI, POI, and an index of Processing Speed.

The Wechsler Intelligence Scale for Children, Version IV (WISC-IV; Wechsler, 2003), is administered to children ranging in age from six years to 16 years. The tests on the WISC-IV are similar in nature to the WPPSI-III, though they are more difficult, as is appropriate for older children. The WISC-IV also includes tests of memory and reasoning that the WPPSI-III does not include. Reflecting these additions, the Full-Scale IQ on the WISC-IV is composed of a Verbal Comprehension Index, a Perceptual Reasoning Index, a Processing Speed Index, and a Working Memory Index.

The Wechsler Adult Intelligence Scale, Version III (WAIS-III Wechsler, 1997) is administered to adults ranging in age from 16 to 89 years, and contains 14 tests. The primary difference between the WAIS-III and its companion scale for children, the WISC-IV, is the inclusion of several tests that assess working memory and more difficult items. The Full-Scale IQ on the WAIS-III is composed of the same indices as that of the WISC-IV. The WAIS-III also provides a Verbal IQ and a Performance IQ.

The boom in intelligence-test construction following the First World War reflected the promise that tests held for matching educational and occupational opportunities to people with particular intellectual capabilities. Although test developers had sometimes quite detailed notions of intellectual capability, tests at this time generally were not created to extend scientific thinking about intelligence. Perhaps for this reason, test developers during this period did not appear to question very frequently whether the tests they had created actually measured what they were supposed to. These tests demonstrated notable practical utility for occupational and educational placement, so it may have been of secondary concern whether they could be considered valid measures of some specific, theory-based notion of intelligence. Advancements in psychological *test theory* in the early 1930s made it possible for psychologists explicitly to link a test of intellectual ability to a particular intelligence theory.

Test Theory

The fundamental goal of test theory is to inform test development by providing methods for evaluating the accuracy, adequacy, coherence, and consistency of a test. Through the use of these methods, test developers can be more certain that they are measuring the intellectual abilities they think they are measuring and can therefore draw more valid conclusions based on test results.

Imagine that a music teacher wants to assess musical aptitude. She believes that a critical aspect of this aptitude is the ability to learn difficult musical compositions. She therefore creates a test that requires her examinees to play two challenging concertos. If a person plays the concertos very well (according to a preset, recognized standard), she concludes that the person has high musical aptitude. If a person plays them poorly, she concludes that the person has low musical aptitude.

Test theory recommends caution before drawing such conclusions. In order to be sure she is truly measuring musical aptitude with her two-concerto test, one question the music teacher must ask herself is *what else* her test might be measuring, besides musical aptitude. For example, exposure to music education would certainly influence how well someone plays the concertos. Would it be fair to conclude that someone who has never had musical instruction has no musical aptitude if she performs the concertos poorly? In addition to musical education, the two-concerto test might also measure the familiarity that different examinees have with the concertos that were chosen. By removing the unwanted factors that her test might also be measuring, the music teacher would improve the accuracy, or *construct validity*, of her test.

She must also ask whether or not performance on her two-concerto test relates to other known indicators of musical aptitude, such as membership in an orchestra or other prestigious musical group. People doing better on her test of musical aptitude should be more likely to be members of musical groups or more likely to be chosen as instructors than people scoring lower on her test. If the music teacher demonstrates that performance on her test corresponds to external (i.e., non-test) criteria associated with the ability it measures, she has demonstrated another aspect of her test's accuracy, its *external validity*.

Another question to ask is what the music teacher's test is *not* measuring that it should be measuring. Playing challenging concertos may not be the only aspect of musical aptitude, which likely also includes ability to sight-read, ability to discern similar notes, sense of rhythm, and so on. The test should include assessments of each of the kinds of performances that reflect musical aptitude, and in proportion to their importance. If ability to sight-read is more important than sense of rhythm, then a greater portion of the test should feature sight-reading tasks than assessments of rhythm. By ensuring that her test adequately samples the aspects of the ability she wishes to measure, the music teacher ensures the *content validity* of her test for measuring that ability.

The concepts of construct validity, external validity, and content validity are important criteria that test developers use to evaluate how precise their measures are. An additional concept of interest is called *reliability*. The reliability of a test is essentially its coherence and consistency. Test problems must represent a coherent sampling of the intellectual ability of interest (i.e., they all measure the same ability), and the results of the test should be relatively consistent over repeated administrations (i.e., the rank order of people's scores should not fluctuate greatly).

Test development efforts after the 1930s were characterized by a more systematic evaluation of the accuracy, adequacy, coherence, and consistency of tests and test problems. As intelligence theories began to multiply, so did the need to evaluate them. Test theory provides a means for carefully constructing assessments precise enough to test scientifically whether or not a particular intelligence theory is valid. Recently adopted methods for analyzing the quality of test problems (Embretson, 1997; Drasgow, Levine & Zickar, 1996) further enhance our ability to construct precise measures of intelligence. Theory-based tests of intelligence, then, can be considered the offspring of the rather prolific coupling of test theory and intelligence theory. As we outlined in

Chapter One, intelligence theories can be traced to the implicit metaphors held by intelligence theorists. Theory-based choices about how to approach intelligence measurement therefore follow directly from implicit metaphors of mind, as we will demonstrate in the section below.

Intelligence Tests and Metaphors of Mind

Geographic metaphor

Intelligence theories based on the geographic metaphor involve identifying the basic ability or set of abilities that supposedly determine the range of intelligent things people can do. Intelligence tests based on this metaphor are therefore designed to assess the ability or abilities theorized to be fundamental to all other intelligent thought.

Single-Factor Tests

Single-factor tests are designed to assess a single, largely general intellectual ability, g (or general intelligence), specified in Spearman's (1927) two-factor theory. Recall from Chapter One that Spearman specified two types of ability factor—g and s—and believed that g was most important for understanding intellectual ability. Spearman (1923) theorized that g was the ability to perceive stimuli and to determine how stimuli are similar and different, and that it was the essence of intelligent behavior. Tests of general intelligence therefore produce a single IQ score that represents this ability, and include problems such as analogies (LAWYER is to CLIENT as DOCTOR is to ??) and series completions (1 3 5 ??). Tests such as Raven's Progressive Matrices (Raven, 1938) or the Cattell Culture Fair Test of g (Cattell & Cattell, 1963) feature sets of geometric figures whose interrelationship must be determined. For example, in one part of the Cattell test, examinees must examine a row of five shapes and determine which two of the five shapes are different from the rest but similar to one another. Though not knowledge-free, figural reasoning tests such as these require relatively less acquired knowledge to complete than other intelligence tests, and are most often used in psychological research. Like the other intelligence tests discussed so far, single-factor tests also have age-appropriate versions, although they are typically administered to groups of examinees at one time and have time limits. Several of the pretheoretical tests described earlier in this chapter (e.g., the Stanford–Binet V) are also considered to be good measures of Spearman's *g* (Jensen, 1980).

Multiple-Factor and Hierarchical-Theory Based Tests

Many of the intelligence tests used today are based on multiple-factor theories and hierarchical theories of intelligence. One of the very first (still published and used today) was the Primary Mental Abilities battery (PMA; Thurstone, 1938), designed to test Thurstone's multiple-factor theory described in Chapter One. In accordance with the theory, the PMA battery measures and provides a separate score for seven abilities: verbal comprehension, verbal fluency (ability to generate verbal material, such as words), mathematical computation and estimation, spatial visualization, inductive reasoning (analogies and syllogisms), perceptual speed, and memory. Like the single-factor tests described above, the tests in the PMA battery are also timed and can be administered to groups of examinees.

Horn and Cattell's (1966) theory of fluid and crystallized abilities serves as the basis for several commonly used intelligence scales. Alan S. Kaufman and Nadeen L. Kaufman have developed a series of such scales, all of which are administered individually and are un-timed. The Kaufman Adolescent and Adult Intelligence Test (KAIT; Kaufman & Kaufman, 1993) is designed for ages 11 to 85 years plus and provides IQ scores for both fluid and crystallized abilities. Recall from Chapter One that fluid ability is defined as flexibility of thought and abstract reasoning capability and that crystallized ability is defined as the accumulation of knowledge and skills. The KAIT tests of fluid abilities assess examinees' ability to decode and use picture-words (analogous to hieroglyphics) and to solve logic problems. The tests of crystallized abilities assess examinees' ability to comprehend oral stories, to infer words with double meanings from a cue for each meaning, and to infer words from a meaning cue and a spelling cue. Four additional, supplemental tests in the scale measure immediate memory and delayed memory.

The Kaufman Brief Intelligence Test (K-BIT; Kaufman & Kaufman, 1990) also provides IQ scores for fluid and crystallized ability, but for purposes of efficiency, includes only one test of each ability. The test measuring fluid ability assesses examinees' ability with figural-reasoning problems. The test measuring crystallized ability assesses examinees' vocabulary and word-definition skills. The K-BIT is designed for ages four to 90 years.

Another commonly used intelligence scale based on Horn and Cattell's theory is the Woodcock–Johnson Psycho-Educational Battery, Version III (WJ-III; Woodcock, McGrew & Mather, 2001). This scale also draws from Carroll's (1993) three-stratum theory, and is designed for people ranging in age from two to over 90 years. Similar to the K-ABC, the WJ-III measures both cognitive ability and academic achievement. The cognitive ability scale contains twenty tests designed to measure several abilities outlined in both Horn and Cattell's and Carroll's hierarchical theories, including short- and long-term memory, working memory, perceptual speed, visual and auditory pattern recognition, comprehension, attention, and reasoning ability. Similar to the tests in the Kaufman series, the WJ-III is also individually administered and untimed. Examinees earn a separate score for verbal ability, thinking ability, and cognitive efficiency, as well as an overall score.

Computational metaphor

Tests of intelligence as defined by computational theories are designed either to measure a single cognitive process believed to be fundamental to intelligent thought (analogous to Spearman's g) or to measure multiple cognitive processes all believed to contribute to intelligent behavior (analogous to multiple ability factors). For this reason, performance on these tests tends to correlate highly with performance on single- and multiple-factor tests of intelligence. The decision regarding what cognitive process to measure is based on the computational intelligence theory espoused by the test developer.

Tests of Working Memory

As described in Chapter One, working memory is one cognitive process believed to be fundamental to intelligence (Kyllonen &

Christal, 1990). Tests of working memory are designed to assess a person's ability to store information in memory while simultaneously performing cognitive operations on that information. There are numerous working memory tests, some of which are featured on the intelligence scales we have already described, such as the WISC-IV and WJ-III. They can be administered either to groups of examinees or in a one-on-one format, and are applicable to a wide range of ages. To keep the discussion of working memory tests within a manageable scope, we will describe three that we believe are representative of the tests commonly used in intelligence assessment and research: Backward Digit Span, ABCD Order (Woltz, 1988), and Operation Span (Turner & Engle, 1989).

In Backward Digit Span, examinees listen to a string of digits and then must repeat the list back in backwards order. A person's span is the largest number of digits he can accurately repeat back. This test and those similar to it are featured on multiple modern intelligence scales, including the WISC-IV, the WAIS-III and the K-ABC.

The ABCD Order test (Woltz, 1988) presents examinees with a series of three statements about the order of four letters, A, B, C, and D, in a string (e.g., if the string is ABCD, one of the statements might be "A precedes B"). Without seeing the letter string, examinees listen to all three statements and then must reproduce the string with the letters in the correct order. A person's score on this test is the number of strings correctly reproduced.

In the Operation Span test (Turner & Engle, 1989) examinees are presented with sets of simple mathematical computations, each of which is associated with a word [e.g., $(7 \times 5) - 2 = 37$? ENGINE]. The examinee must evaluate the correctness of each computation in a set while holding the word associated with it in memory. Set size varies from two computation/word pairings to five. After evaluating all of the computations in a set, the examinee must recall the words associated with each one. A person's operation span is the maximum size of the set from which he can recall all of the words, while also accurately evaluating the computations. This test is analogous to the Reading Span test, in which the examinee reads a set of sentences and, after finishing reading all of the sentences in the set, must recall the last word of each sentence (Daneman & Carpenter, 1980).

Cognitive Assessment System (CAS)

The CAS (Naglieri & Das, 1997) is an intelligence scale that assesses four cognitive processes believed to be critical to intellectual functioning and associated with specific regions of the brain: planning, sustained selective attention, information integration, and information ordering (Das, Kirby & Jarman, 1979; Das, Naglieri & Kirby, 1994; Luria, 1973, 1980). The tests of planning on this scale require that examinees create and use effective plans to solve test problems. An example of a planning task in the CAS is the Visual Search task, in which examinees must scan through a set of letters or numbers on a page for a target letter or number. Faster identification of the target depends on the efficiency of the plan that the examinee has formed for searching the page (Das, Naglieri & Kirby, 1994). The tests of sustained selective attention require examinees to attend to a stimulus while ignoring other stimuli, for example identifying numbers on a page when they appear in one form (e.g., **bold**) but not in another (e.g., not bold; Das, Naglieri & Kirby, 1994). Information integration is assessed by test problems that require the examinee to integrate pieces of information into a meaningful whole, such as matching a picture to a verbal description (e.g., "the ball in a basket on the table," p. 111, Das, Naglieri & Kirby, 1994). Information ordering is assessed by test problems that require the examinee to order information in a particular way for solving test problems. One example of a CAS test requiring information ordering is called Sentence Repetition, where the examinee must repeat a sentence with complete accuracy back to the person who presented it (Das, Naglieri & Kirby, 1994). The CAS is individually administered to people ranging in age from five to 17 years, and provides a separate score for each of the four cognitive processes plus an overall score.

Cognitive Abilities Measurement (CAM) Battery

The CAM Battery (Kyllonen, 1993) also assesses multiple cognitive processes. In addition to breadth of general knowledge, the CAM battery measures working memory, information-processing speed, and ability to learn simple, novel rules for classifying information. Examinees receive a score for their performance on each of the four parts of this test battery. This battery is intended for adults, specifically U.S. Air Force recruits, who range in age from approximately 18 to 30 years, and is administered to large groups of examinees via a computer. The CAM Battery is not commercially available, but it has been administered to several thousand U.S. Air Force recruits for research purposes.

Biological metaphor

Intelligence assessment based in the biological metaphor typically involves tests drawn from other metaphors, primarily the geographic and computational metaphors. This reliance on tests drawn from other metaphors stems from the fact that researchers using the biological approach work backwards from already-developed intelligence tests to understand the neurological basis of performance on those tests. That is, intelligence must be defined *before* exploration of neurological functions is conducted, rather than the other way around. As an example, when positron emission tomography (PET) or functional magnetic resonance imaging (fMRI) is used to explore brain activity during intellectual tasks, the task is often a test of intelligence based on another metaphor, such as Raven's Progressive Matrices or tests of working memory.

One exception can be found in the work of John Duncan and his colleagues (Duncan et al., 2000), who created their own tests of intelligence to determine which of two intelligence theories — Spearman's or Thomson's (see Chapter One) — could be better supported by neurological data. Specifically, Duncan and his colleagues created tests that they believed to be strong measures of Spearman's g and tests that they believed did not measure g as well. The two types of test were similar in all other respects, so that when Duncan and his colleagues identified differences in blood flow between the two types of test, they could attribute the differences to the use of general intelligence. They argued that if blood flow during the use of g is relatively confined to a particular area of the brain, then such evidence would support Spearman's theory. In contrast, if blood flow were relatively diffuse across brain regions, then such evidence would support Thomson's theory.

Another possible exception might be the Cognitive Assessment System (CAS), described above, because it is based on a theory

(Luria, 1973, 1980) that explicitly specifies regions in the brain that underlie the four cognitive processes tested by the CAS battery: planning (frontal cortex), sustained selective attention (brain stem and midbrain structures), and information integration and information ordering (temporal, parietal, and occipital lobes). Luria believed that each of the three cortical regions was highly differentiated from the others but that they worked together to produce thought and action of various kinds. The developers of the CAS system warn, however, that the CAS should not be used to assess deficits neurological functioning (Das, Naglieri & Kirby, 1994).

The Kaufman Assessment Battery for Children (K-ABC; Kaufman & Kaufman, 1983) is also based on neurological theory (e.g., Das, Kirby & Jarman, 1979). It is designed for ages two-and-a-half to twelve-and-a-half years and measures both the sequential and simultaneous processing of information, as well as academic achievement. The tests of sequential processing assess, among other things, children's ability to solve test problems by arranging test stimuli in a sequential or serial order (e.g., recalling a set of numbers in the order in which they were presented). The tests of simultaneous processing assess, among other things, children's ability to discover analogical relationships by synthesizing and integrating information (e.g., solving figural analogies problems as in the Cattell test). Like the other Kaufman scales described previously, the K-ABC is administered individually and untimed.

Epistemological metaphor

Intelligence testing based on the epistemological metaphor primarily stems from the early work done by Piaget. As described in Chapter One, Piaget was fundamentally interested in how the cognitive and knowledge structures of children change as they become intellectually more competent. He therefore developed a series of tasks based on his four stages of development to test whether children possessed the structures expected for a given age.

To assess whether a child has acquired the necessary cognitive and knowledge structures to be considered in the sensorimotor stage, an examiner might test whether an infant searches for an object hidden from view. This is the stage during which children learn that objects exist even if unseen, so searching for hidden objects indicates a correct response to the task.

To assess achievement of preoperational thinking, when children's thinking is expected to become less egocentric, the examiner might conduct the *Three Mountains Experiment*. In this experiment, the child is asked to describe a papier-mâché model of three mountains from a visual perspective different from his own (e.g., the perspective of a doll that is placed on the other side of the model). If the child can describe the model from another's perspective, he has produced a correct response.

Piaget hypothesized that children in the concrete operations stage learn the concept of conservation (i.e., that changes in the appearance of a quantity do not change the quantity itself). He developed a series of tasks to test conservation assessing, for example, whether children who poured the same amount of fluid from one container to another (with a different shape) could tell that the volume had been preserved. If the children could tell that volume had been preserved, they performed correctly on the task.

Piaget believed that scientific thinking is the hallmark of intellectual development. Therefore, for the final, formal operations stage he presented adolescents with tasks to challenge their scientific thinking. The pendulum task, for instance, was designed to assess whether an adolescent takes a methodical or an unsystematic approach to identifying the variable (e.g., weight of object) that determines how long it takes the pendulum to complete one swing. Demonstrating more systematic, scientific thinking allowed the adolescent to "pass" the task.

An important aspect of Piaget's tasks is the verbal exchange between the examiner and the examinee, which guides the measurement process. Through this exchange, the examiner presents the examinee with the task requirements and the examinee communicates and justifies his answers. Another important aspect of these tasks is that children do not earn an overall score that represents the number of tasks they perform correctly. Piaget was not interested in comparing children's capabilities but instead in characterizing the developmental process of cognitive ability, so scores were not of particular use to him.

Perhaps because Piaget was not interested in testing, per se, his tasks in their original form have not been developed into a stand-alone test of intelligence. They are incorporated, however, in the Kaufman Adult Intelligence Test (KAIT) described previously. Efforts have also been made to translate Piaget's tasks into test problems that are more typical of standardized, commercially available intelligence tests (e.g., Tuddenham, 1969, 1971). Tuddenham, in particular, sought to create Piagetian tasks that largely eliminated the verbal exchange between examiner and examinee. In Piagetian tasks created in such a way, the quality of examinee responses could be objectively determined and scored, rather than inferred by the examiner. Such tasks also took less time to administer. Tuddenham's test focused on measuring the transition from pre-operational thought to concrete-operational thought, though it was never made into a commercially available test. Experimentally, performance on Piagetian tasks and tests has shown a close relationship to general intelligence as defined by Spearman (e.g., Humphreys & Parsons, 1979; Humphreys, Rich & Davey, 1985).

Piaget's successors, the neo-Piagetians, have developed assessment tasks of their own, which are similar in spirit but modified in design. These modifications arose in part from the fact that Piaget's experiments proved difficult to administer to children of different cultures and did not take into account the specific knowledge that children acquire from their experiences. For example, a child might demonstrate formal operational thought in a social domain but not in, say, a mathematical domain, due to less exposure to mathematical reasoning or knowledge.

Sociological metaphor

Examinations of how various socialization practices, such as parenting styles, affect intelligence typically involve intelligence tests based on the geographic metaphor or tests of school achievement. However, Vygotsky's interest in the difference between a person's ability to do something unassisted versus assisted has had interesting implications for the measurement of intelligence.

Imagine two children who perform equally poorly on a test of long division because it is just out of reach of their current level of mathematical ability. On a typical math test, these children would earn the same score. Now consider what might happen if both children were provided with guided assistance in how to solve long-division problems. One child is able to arrive at correct solutions with this help while the other child fails to do so. Likely one would conclude that the mathematical ability of these two children differs. Intelligence tests that measure people's unassisted performance may treat two people with different learning potentials as if they had the same mental capability, which could be misleading.

For this reason, Vygotsky's thinking has led to the development of a very different kind of intelligence-testing practice, called *dynamic testing*, which captures an individual's learning potential as opposed to his intellectual performance at a given point of time. Dynamic tests of intelligence measure a person's performance on various intelligence tests both before and after a brief instructional intervention, and the difference between these two performances is taken to be an indicator of learning potential. The use of dynamic tests has been explored in a variety of contexts, particularly in testing the intelligence of children with various cognitive disabilities.

Two commonly used dynamic tests are the Learning Potential Assessment Device (LPAD), based on Feuerstein's (1980) thinking, and Swanson's Cognitive Processing Test (S-CPT). The LPAD involves primarily geographic intelligence tests, such as Raven's Progressive Matrices, and tests three aspects of learning potential. The first aspect is *modality*—the different senses (i.e., vision, hearing) in which learning potential can be expressed. The second aspect is level of complexity or novelty of the situations the learner must handle. The third aspect is the different cognitive operations (e.g., memory, divergent thinking, evaluation) for which the learner can show different levels of potential. For example, a person may show greater learning potential on simple tasks that require memory for aurally presented words than on more novel tasks that require divergent thinking with pictures. The examiner plays a critical role in the testing process by detecting failures to demonstrate learning potential and determining the best way to remedy these failures. An important function of the LPAD is the identification of particular cognitive deficits in order to provide intervention outside of the testing situation.

The S-CPT is based on the assumption of the centrality of working memory to human intelligence. It features eleven tests, which can be administered together as a battery or separately to measure information-processing potential (Swanson, 1995a). The S-CPT is administered to children, who earn seven scores on the test (Swanson, 1995b). The different scores amount to indices of the child's best performance (a) before intervention (a pre-test score); (b) during intervention; and (c) after intervention (a post-test score), as well as the difference between (d) the child's performance before help and while receiving help; and (e) the child's performance before help and after help. Children also earn a score for (f) how many prompts they required during intervention to earn their best score; and (g) a score for the efficiency of the memory strategy they used on particular subtests of the scale.

These and several other dynamic tests (see Sternberg & Grigorenko, 2002) hold great promise for assessing the kind of learning potential that static tests of intelligence do not. However, the information about people's learning potential that comes from dynamic testing has not yet proved to add much to the information that static intelligence tests, such as those described earlier in this chapter, already provide.

Anthropological metaphor

The anthropological metaphor is not associated with particular intelligence tests. Instead of having implications for *what* exactly an intelligence test should measure, anthropological theories of intelligence have implications for *how* intelligence tests should be designed. Because culture is seen as central to intelligence, intelligence is not generally believed to be universal but to be a different thing in different cultures. According to many anthropological theories, therefore, an intelligence test should be designed to assess the abilities valued and developed in the culture whose members are being assessed. To assess abilities that are believed to be shared across multiple cultures, tests must be carefully designed such that the same ability is measured in the different cultures (Greenfield, 1997).

Although much cross-cultural research on intelligence has been conducted, there have been relatively few systematic attempts to create tests of intelligence that measure the same abilities across cultures and even fewer attempts to rigorously evaluate the cross-cultural equivalence of these tests. Sternberg and his colleagues (Sternberg, Nokes, Geissler, et al., 2001) made one such attempt. They developed a test of practical intelligence for children living in Kenya in order to explore the applicability of aspects of the theory of successful intelligence (Sternberg, 1997, see also Chapter One) to a non-Western culture. Although they did not specifically evaluate the cross-cultural equivalence of tests of practical intelligence, they did demonstrate that analytical and practical intelligence are distinct mental capabilities in both Western and non-Western cultures. Later research has explicitly examined the cross-cultural equivalence of a practical intelligence test, finding that with relatively simple translation the same test of practical intelligence measured roughly the same ability both in Spain and the United States. (Cianciolo, Grigorenko, Jarvin, Gil, Drebot & Sternberg, under review).

Systems metaphor

Intelligence assessments based on systems theories are designed to capture multiple aspects of intelligence. In sharp contrast to single-metaphor assessments, which typically target aptitudes valued in school settings, systems-metaphor assessments target a wide range of aptitudes, including those valued in everyday-life situations. The promise of systems tests of intelligence is that they capture intelligence more broadly and, perhaps, more equitably for people in traditionally disadvantaged groups. The limitation of such assessments is that they are difficult to create. Of the three systems theories described in Chapter One, only Sternberg's Triarchic Theory of Successful Intelligence has an associated intelligence test (Sternberg, 1991; Sternberg & The Rainbow Project Collaborators, in press), although it is not yet commercially available.

Sternberg Triarchic Abilities Test (STAT)

Consistent with Sternberg's theory, this un-timed group-administered test is designed to measure analytical, creative, and practical abilities in adolescents using both multiple-choice and essay/performance questions. These three abilities are assessed in three different content domains, verbal, quantitative, and figural.

Analytic–Verbal problems require the examinee to infer the meaning of a new word (e.g., "yip") from the context of a paragraph in which it is embedded. *Analytic–Quantitative* problems present the examinee with a series of numbers, and the examinee must determine the number that comes next. In *Analytic–Figural* problems, examinees must identify the missing piece of a matrix figure. An essay question is also used to assess analytical ability. Examinees must write an analysis of the advantages and disadvantages of having police or security guards in a school building.

Creative–Verbal problems require examinees to solve verbal analogies preceded by counterfactual premises (e.g., "lions eat slippers" → "SLIPPER is to LION as GRASS is to ?? (a) WEEDS (b) SHEEP (c) GREEN"). *Creative–Quantitative* problems require examinees to fill in number matrices by inferring the number that corresponds to a novel symbol (e.g., $* + 7 = 15$). In *Creative–Figural* problems, examinees must apply a transformation rule inferred from one set of figures to another. Creative ability is also assessed by brief written and oral stories, by a captioning task in which examinees provide a caption for modified cartoons, and by an essay in which examinees describe how they would reform their school system to produce an ideal one.

Practical–Verbal problems require the examinee to engage in everyday reasoning to solve problems typical in the life of an adolescent. In *Practical–Quantitative* problems, examinees must solve math problems presented in scenarios requiring the use of math in everyday life. *Practical–Figural* problems require participants to use a map of an area (e.g., a subway system) for planning routes. Practical ability is also assessed using brief scenarios that present examinees with a problem typically faced in the everyday life. Examinees must rate the quality of several possible responses for handling the problem situation. Also, a practical essay requires examinees to state a problem in their life and present three practical solutions for solving it.

An examinee's score on the STAT has two parts. The first part reflects the examinee's level of analytical, creative, and practical ability as assessed by multiple-choice problems. The second part reflects the examinee's level of analytical, creative, and practical ability as assessed by open-ended, or performance, problems. Analytical, creative, and practical scores on these two parts can be combined and summed for an overall score.

Recent Advances in Testing

The advent of the microcomputer has been critically important in advancing the efficiency of group intelligence testing — making administration, scoring, and data storage tasks much easier. It has also led to advances in the testing process itself. For example, simple tests of motor skills that previously were too difficult to administer to more than one person at a time can now be administered to groups of 10 people or more using touchscreen technology (Ackerman & Cianciolo, 1999). In addition, tests can now be created so that examinees need only complete problems that correspond to their ability level, rather than having to suffer through many items that are either too easy or too hard. This method for administering tests is called *computerized adaptive testing*, and is now being used by the Educational Testing Service to administer the SAT and GRE.

More sophisticated statistical analysis software has permitted very important advances in the design of more typical intelligence test problems. Among other things, test developers can now evaluate how well the difficulty of particular test items corresponds to the ability level of the examinees for whom a test is intended (Drasgow, Levine & Zickar, 1996). Such an evaluation allows test administrators to select problems before testing that will provide the best measurement for a person of a particular ability level. It also informs the computerized adaptive testing administration method described above, in which computers select the "best-measuring" items while the examinee takes the test. Whether intelligence tests are administered in group format, via one-on-one testing, or on computers, challenges to the practice of intelligence testing still remain.

Controversy Surrounding Intelligence Testing

Controversy has surrounded intelligence testing almost since its inception (see Carroll, 1982). This controversy arose despite initial hope that the practice of making educational and occupational decisions based on intelligence test scores would be a democratic alternative to nepotism or other discriminatory practices. First, many people had concerns that the tests created to measure intelligence were actually measuring one's knowledge of the dominant culture. They worried that students who performed poorly on these tests could be placed into special education and labeled as retarded when in fact they may simply have been members of an ethnic minority (Carroll, 1982). Indeed, the successful lawsuit, *Larry P.* v. *Wilson Riles* (1979), was filed because black students were alleged to be highly over-represented in classes for the mildly retarded due to their intelligence-test scores. Concerns about cultural bias in intelligence testing and the interpretation of test results still exist today (Helms, 1997), though some argue that such concerns are unjustified (Jensen, 1980; Rushton & Jensen, in press).

A second concern stemmed from apparent disagreement between the public and intelligence theorists as to what should be considered intelligent. Many of the intelligence tests used historically and currently for diagnostic and placement purposes are based on the geographic metaphor, in which intelligence is believed to be a highly abstract, very general capability that gives the people who have more of it an advantage in most tasks over those who have less. Implicit theories of intelligence held by many laypeople, however, coincide more with a systems metaphor in that they believe intelligent behavior involves not just abstract thinking, but everyday thinking as well (Sternberg, Conway, Ketron & Bernstein, 1981). Having such implicit theories can lead to the view that intelligence is not being completely captured by the dominant testing practices. That intelligence tests are not better predictors of performance in school and on the job suggests that there is likely some truth to this view.

The controversy over intelligence-test content that began in the 1920s is still going strong today, and has resulted in a substantial reduction in the use of intelligence testing by employers and public-school educators (although the opposite trend has occurred in achievement testing). One noteworthy result of this controversy is that several types of intelligence tests, based on metaphors other than the geographic, have been created. Some of these tests, such as the CAS, tests of working memory, and the STAT, as well as dynamic-testing practices, have reached the public and may serve to resolve some of the thorny issues associated with intelligence testing.

Conclusion

In this chapter we have presented early attempts to measure intelligent functioning and discussed how test theory led to a transition in thinking about intelligence testing. We also described several intelligence tests that are linked to particular metaphors of mind, highlighting how beliefs about the nature of intelligence are reflected in test content. We discussed recent advances in intelligence testing that have stemmed from the use of computers, including the assessment of new competencies and the analysis of test problems. Finally, we briefly summarized controversy surrounding what intelligence tests measure and how they are used.

An additional controversy associated with intelligence research involves debate over whether intelligence is an innate, immutable characteristic of people (e.g., see Sternberg, 1998). In the next chapter, we will present several approaches to improve intelligence and discuss how they relate to particular metaphors of mind. Just as each metaphor has implications for how intelligence should be measured, each has implications for how it should be taught.

CHAPTER THREE

The Teaching of Intelligence

Suppose our three blind men from Chapters One and Two wanted to make a particular animal more elephant-like. The approaches taken by these men, and perhaps their relative success, would depend on what the men had determined to be the nature of elephants. The man who thought elephants are snake-like might increase the agility and strength of the animal's trunk or tail through a rigorous exercise regimen. The man who thought that elephants are like walls might attempt to increase the height and width of the creature through the use of dietary supplements and more frequent feedings. Finally, the man who thought that elephants are like trees might attempt to increase the diameter of the creature's legs by feeding it muscle-enhancing hormones.

Approaches to improving intelligence can be linked to metaphors of mind, just as can the theories of intelligence on which they are based. In this chapter, we describe the unique characteristics of teaching for intelligence and we review a history of approaches to teaching intelligence. We start from Alfred Binet's intellectual exercises for retarded children and finish with recent theory-based programs, such as those of Robert J. Sternberg and Howard Gardner.

Just as tests of intelligence and tests of academic achievement can appear to be quite similar (see Chapter Two), attempts to teach intelligence and to teach academic knowledge and skills can be difficult to distinguish. That is, the design of instructional interventions created to enhance intelligence is often quite similar to the design of standard educational practices. A curriculum first is determined, students then participate in the curriculum, and finally (in ideal circumstances) a rigorous evaluation of what was learned is conducted. If students demonstrate increased facility with the topic that was taught, one generally infers that the curriculum was successful. Importantly, both intelligence instruction and educational practices are based on the assumption that, with guidance, improvement can occur.

There are, however, some important differences between teaching intelligence and teaching typical school subjects. The first difference is that interventions designed to improve intelligence generally do not focus on improving a particular academic skill, such as mathematics or reading comprehension. Rather, the teaching of intelligence focuses on enhancing general mental faculties, such as reasoning or problem solving, which are useful in many diverse academic subjects. Consequently, instruction for increasing intelligence can be delivered either via stand-alone courses or through infusion into ongoing classroom practices.

The second difference is that the evaluation of interventions designed to improve intelligence involves intelligence testing, rather than (or in addition to) tests of academic achievement. The choice of intelligence test used to determine the success of a particular intervention generally stems from the theory of intelligence espoused by the person who designed the intervention. Ideally, there is a theoretical correspondence between the topics covered by the curriculum and the tests used to evaluate learning outcomes (i.e., they are based on the same metaphor for conceptualizing the nature of intelligence).

The final difference is that the positive effects of teaching intelligence are expected to extend beyond performance on a particular intelligence test. Although a physics instructor would likely not expect his students to write better poems because of his teaching, an intelligence instructor would expect her students not only to perform better the intelligence tests featured in her intervention, but also on intelligence tests that were not used as part of her intervention. Otherwise, the instructor may only conclude that she has "taught to the test," rather than having actually improved intelligence.

Attempts to improve intelligence, as is shown throughout the rest of this chapter, all share this distinctiveness from standard educational practices. The teaching of intelligence has often been closely tied to schools, however, because intelligence has long been thought to be an important determinant of school success. Indeed, some of the earliest approaches to teaching intelligence focused primarily on preparing children for school, particularly children considered at a disadvantage with regard to such preparation.

Early Approaches

The improvement of intelligence has been a topic of much interest for as long as intelligence has been formally evaluated, as can be seen in the efforts of Alfred Binet. As described in Chapter Two, Binet and his colleagues (Binet & Simon, 1916) believed that intelligence is a set of well-developed judgment skills that children must apply in order to benefit from education. Binet therefore believed that intelligence could be improved through the enhancement of judgment skills and that, by improving his intelligence, a formerly retarded child could enjoy success in standard education. This view was in sharp contrast to that of Binet's contemporary, Francis Galton (1883), who believed that intelligence was innate and not changeable.

Binet ([1909] 1975) proposed a set of simple exercises, which he called *mental orthopedics*, to enhance the school readiness of retarded students. He likened mental orthopedics to physical orthopedics, saying, "Just as physical orthopedics correct a curvature of the thoracic spine, mental orthopedics straighten, cultivate, fortify such mental abilities as attention, memory, perception, judgment, the will" (p. 111). For one year, Binet and his colleagues worked with a class of retarded students, exposing them to various exercises that could be performed either in the home or in school settings, and were not specific to particular academic subjects. One of the first exercises — for developing will — was called "playing statue," in which the teacher signaled the children to freeze in place for a specified length of time before resuming normal classroom activities. The duration of immobility began with a few seconds and increased to one minute over the course of the year. Binet's other methods for developing will and discipline featured exercises of speed and motor skills. Exercises for developing other mental faculties, including perception, observation, memory, imagination, invention, analysis, judgment, followed exercises of will. One of these exercises involved showing the children a board with several objects glued to it. After being allowed to view the board for five seconds, the children were then asked to write down as many objects as they could remember. Binet found that after one year in his mental orthopedics program, the retarded children advanced their school performance by two years.

Binet was passionate about improving children's ability to benefit from formal education by helping them learn how to learn. He felt it was "a serious matter for all of us, for society" (ibid., p. 105) that children entering school with inadequate intellectual skills were not getting the remedial education they required. Although Binet's mental orthopedics exercises are used only on an informal basis today, widely known programs such as Project Head Start carry on the tradition of intervention in the lives of young children requiring educational assistance. With a projected 2003 budget of over 6.5 billion dollars (U.S. Department of Health & Human Services, 2003), the Head Start program exemplifies two things: (a) the importance placed by United States' society on efforts to improve children's educability, and (b) the strength of the belief in the United States that such efforts can be successful.

The federally funded Head Start program began in 1965 as part of the United States' government's "War on Poverty." The stated goal of Head Start was to improve the social, emotional, physical, and cognitive development of children living in poverty before they entered the school system so that they could enjoy the same benefits from education as their more privileged peers. Children participating in the current Head Start program range in age from three to five years, with even younger children participating in the newly established Early Head Start Program (U.S. Department of Health & Human Services, 2003). Nearly all Head Start children live below the poverty level, and thirteen percent of enrollees in 2001–2002 had a disability of some kind (U.S. Department of Health & Human Services, 2003). The format of Head Start interventions varies from being based entirely on home visits to being based entirely in a classroom. Some interventions combine classroom instruction with home visits.

There does not exist a nationwide, standardized Head Start curriculum. Moreover, organizations awarded grants to implement a Head Start intervention in a particular community need not structure their curriculum around a particular theory of intelligence, and most do not. Instead, Head Start interventions for teaching intelligence generally have been designed to facilitate children's language acquisition and to improve their performance on intelligence test-like tasks. The intelligence of Head Start children typically is measured by using tests of IQ, such as the Stanford–Binet V or the WPPSI-III, which are not associated with a particular theory of intelligence but do provide a reasonable estimate of general intelligence, as defined by Spearman (see Chapter One).

Project Head Start came under fire from the second Bush administration, because of its desire to shift the responsibility of funding and managing Head Start from the federal government to state governments (Bumiller, 2003). Reluctance to continue using federal funds to support Head Start appears to come from long-standing concerns about the effectiveness of compensatory education in improving the intellectual capability of its enrollees (e.g., see Jensen, 1969; Lazar & Darlington, 1982; Washington & Bailey, 1995). Interestingly, although IQ scores have been increasing over the past several decades (on average about three points every 10 years, see Flynn, 1987), developing instructional methods that can improve an individual person's IQ score has proven to be more difficult. Improvements in IQ scores achieved by Head Start enrollees have been approximately seven points or less, and do not appear to last once the children have spent a few years in school. Improving intellectual functioning is only one aspect of Head Start's mission, however, and is of secondary interest relative to the development of social and emotional adjustment (Washington, 1987; Zigler & Styfco, 1993). Children enrolled in the Head Start program have demonstrated improved attitudes toward school performance, reduced likelihood of repeating years of schooling, and reduced enrollment in special education courses (Lazar & Darlington, 1982).

In these early, non-theory-based approaches to teaching intelligence, intelligence was roughly conceptualized as the ability to use sound judgment and to learn from experience, and was measured using various tests of IQ. More recent attempts to teach intelligence have been more systematic in their approach and have had specific ties to theory, which may account for their relatively greater success. They were designed around conceptualizations of intelligence that can be linked to the metaphors we have described in the first two chapters. The particular theory on which an attempt to teach intelligence is based has implications for how intelligence is assessed, where improvements in intelligence are sought, and what the targets for instruction will be.

Theory-Based Approaches

Geographic metaphor

At first, designing methods for teaching intelligence according to the geographic metaphor seems simple. It is clear that to be consistent with geographic theorizing about intelligence, geographic approaches to teaching intelligence should seek to improve people's basic intellectual abilities. Different approaches should be distinguished by their basis in a different geographic intelligence theory. For example, an instructional intervention based on Spearman's (1927) theory should target the general intelligence factor, or g. The effectiveness of the intervention should be evaluated by examining scores on a test of general intelligence, such as Raven's Progressive Matrices. If scores on the Raven's test and, importantly, other tests of general intelligence, go up — and stay up — one can then conclude the intervention was successful at increasing intelligence.

Things become more difficult when one tries to use geographic theories of intelligence to design a curriculum that could accomplish such a feat. This is because geographic theories identify what abilities people may have, but they do not explain what exactly these abilities are in terms of cognitive processes or strategies (see Chapter One). As an analogy, imagine a person faced with the task of increasing his *norbert*. This person does not know exactly what *norbert* is, but he does know that certain kinds of situations call for having it, such as driving a car while talking on the phone and grocery shopping with a child. Not knowing what *norbert* is, this person decides to expose himself to as many *norbert*-demanding situations as he can in order to get some practice and hopefully improve. Similarly, methods for increasing intelligence in which the design is based strictly on a geographic theory of intelligence would involve providing pupils with experience practicing items on geographic-theory-based intelligence tests or engaging pupils in test-like games or activities.

One attempt to use geographic intelligence theory for designing intelligence instruction was made by Mary N. Meeker and her colleagues (Meeker, 1969; Meeker & Mestyanek, 1976). Like Binet, Meeker stressed the importance of teaching children how to learn, which she believed could be accomplished by trying to improve the particular abilities where children experienced difficulty. Meeker used Guilford's (1956) structure-of-intellect (SOI) theory as a basis for determining what abilities should be measured and developed in gifted children in order for them to achieve maximal educational success. It was stated in Chapter One that there were 120 abilities in Guilford's (1956) initial theory. Each ability had a different content (figural, symbolic, semantic, or behavioral), cognitive product (units, classes, relations, systems, transformations, or implications), and mental operation (cognition, memory, divergent production, convergent production, or evaluation) component. One of these abilities might be, for example, *memory for semantic units*, measured by a test of word recall.

On the basis of scores derived from 17 short tests of SOI abilities, Meeker developed a method for constructing ability profiles for children, which were then used to determine what the remedial education for each child should be (Valett, 1978). Meeker developed several games, activities, and curriculum materials that could be selected to remedy children's particular intellectual weaknesses. One game, intended to develop memory for words, was called "password." In this game, children pair off, and one child is given a card with a word on it. The other child then tries to figure out what word is on the card, using one-word clues given to her by her partner. Initial evaluations of Meeker's methods indicated that they were somewhat successful. Children performed better on SOI ability tests after participating in the SOI program, with especially notable improvements demonstrated by retarded children (Valett, 1978).

In 2004, approximately 2,000 educators and clinicians practicing in the United States have been trained using SOI methods. They are involved in implementing the Bridges program, which was developed in the mid-1980s and based on Meeker's original ideas. Bridges focuses on the remediation of a wider set of intellectual weaknesses than was addressed in the original SOI program. In addition, the Bridges program provides vocational counseling to secondary students on the basis of their SOI ability profiles. There have been positive evaluations of the effectiveness of the Bridges program, but the data have not been published at the time of going to press, so it is not possible to make a definitive statement about the benefits of this program (see Tracey, 2003).

Many psychologists who endorse geographic theories of intelligence seem not to believe intelligence can be modified, which may explain why there have been relatively few attempts to increase intelligence as defined by the geographic metaphor. Perhaps more importantly, the geographic metaphor does not provide a tremendous amount of guidance with regard to teaching intelligence. It is likely that the person in the analogy we described above would have had more success if he understood that *norbert* was the ability to divide attention across multiple competing demands and to react quickly to changing events. He could then have provided himself with a systematically designed set of exercises specifically to improve these skills. Many psychologists who seek to improve people's basic intellectual abilities similarly provide systematically designed sets of exercises for their pupils. The design of these exercises is frequently based on computational theories of intelligence, which attempt to explain the cognitive processes underlying intellectual abilities and to identify the strategies necessary for performing well on intelligence tests.

Computational metaphor

Some of the earliest computational approaches to teaching intelligence involved training people to perform better on the kinds of problems found on tests of intelligence as geographically defined. First, test problems — often some form of analogy — were analyzed in order to determine the cognitive processes that were required to complete the problems correctly. Next, strategies for quickly and accurately executing the required cognitive processes were identified. People were then trained to use the strategies, and post-training performance on intelligence tests was evaluated. Numerous studies were conducted using this computational training approach, both to identify the basic cognitive processes involved in intelligence (e.g., Brown & Campione, 1978; Holzman, Glaser & Pellegrino, 1976; see the cognitive-training approach described in Chapter One) and to explore intellectual competency and the teachability of intelligence (e.g., Baltes & Willis, 1982; Herrnstein, Nickerson, de Sánchez & Swets, 1987; Sternberg, Ketron & Powell, 1982).

One notable attempt to improve intelligence as measured by the geographic metaphor was called Project Intelligence (Herrnstein, Nickerson, de Sánchez & Swets, 1987). This experimental course, which took place during the 1982-3 academic school year, involved 463 Venezuelan seventh graders who received 56 lessons covering cognitive competencies believed to be fundamental to intelligence. These competencies included reasoning, understanding language, problem solving, decision making, and inventive thinking. The student's regular teachers, who had been trained extensively in the course materials, taught the experimental course.

Before and after instruction, students took several intelligence tests and tests of general academic achievement. Students who participated in the course showed a significantly greater increase in scores on the academic achievement tests than did students who did not participate in the course. Similarly, there was a greater increase in scores on the intelligence tests for course participants than for nonparticipants, although this increase was statistically significant for only a small subset of these tests. Unfortunately, Project Intelligence, like other similar projects, was terminated by the Venezuelan government before long-term effects of the instruction could be assessed. The reason was that the governing party that had supported the research was voted out of office, having lost to a party whose campaign promise was to eliminate programs such as Project Intelligence, which they mocked and viewed as a waste of government money.

Another attempt was that of Paul B. Baltes, Sherry L. Willis and their colleagues (see Baltes & Willis, 1982), called the Penn State Adult Development and Enrichment Project (Project ADEPT). A series of studies from Project ADEPT were designed to enhance the intellectual capability, specifically the fluid intelligence, of older adults from 60 to 80 years of age. Defined in Chapter One as one's flexibility of thought and abstract reasoning capability, fluid intelligence declines with age, making coping with unfamiliar problem situations more difficult for older adults. Baltes, Willis, and their colleagues sought to determine whether the fluid intelligence of older adults could be improved with training.

One of the Project ADEPT studies involved training 58 older adults to improve their performance in test problems involving figural reasoning (Willis, Blieszner & Baltes, 1981). The training consisted of five, one-hour training sessions, which featured practice on the relational rules (e.g., size, shape) determined to be important for solving figural reasoning problems such as those presented on the Raven test. Similarly, another study involved training 52 older adults to reason better on test problems involving induction (Blieszner, Willis & Baltes, 1981). The training in this study also consisted of five, one-hour sessions, but instead featured practice on identifying the patterns that could be present in inductive reasoning test problems, such as the odd-number sequence in the following number series problem: 1 3 5 ???. The results from both of these studies indicated that older adults who participated in the training demonstrated substantial increases in performance on related tests of fluid intelligence. The benefits of induction training did not appear to last beyond six months, however.

Another, relatively more recently explored, kind of computational approach to improving intelligence focuses on enhancing thinking skills more generally, and has its origins in the thinking of philosopher John Dewey (1933). Dewey believed that reflective thought — the critical analysis of one's ideas and behaviors — was an important aspect of good thinking skills. He outlined phases of reflective thought, which have familiar counterparts in what modern psychologists now call the "problem-solving process." These phases include recognizing that a problem must be solved, defining what the problem is, testing the validity of one's definition of the problem by taking action or by further thought, revising one's understanding of the problem based on the test and, finally, evaluation of the revised problem definition.

Numerous philosophers and psychologists have sought to understand people's general thinking and problem-solving skills (e.g., Ennis, 1987) and to enhance intelligence and school performance by improving them (Andrade & Perkins, 1998; Baron & Sternberg, 1987; Davidson & Sternberg, 1984; Lipman, 1993; Nickerson, 1989). The methods used by these scholars have ranged widely — from using stories to engage children in the philosophical analysis of problems (Philosophy for Children; see Lipman, 1987, 1993) to training the particular cognitive processes involved in insight and learning from context (Davidson & Sternberg, 1984; Sternberg, 1987) to exploring complex problems by discussing multiple points of view (Paul, 1987).

One of the more recent approaches put forward is that of David N. Perkins and his colleagues (Andrade & Perkins, 1998; Grotzer

& Perkins, 2000), called Cognitive Reorganization (CORE). CORE is designed to enhance thinking in five areas: (1) the thinking strategies people use to solve problems; (2) the methods people use to monitor their thought processes; (3) people's thinking tendencies and attitudes towards thinking; (4) the technological and social supports people use for thinking; and (5) the methods people use to extend their thinking to new situations. CORE methods are designed to teach students to think more deeply about problems before solving them, to monitor their thinking more closely, to be more open, careful, and organized about their thinking, to draw upon multiple resources for thinking, and to make better connections between past, present, and future thinking experiences.

The evaluation of programs designed to teach thinking skills has been mired in difficulty (Grotzer & Perkins, 2000). It is difficult to conduct studies that can adequately test this kind of intervention because they involve the long-term investment of teachers, school districts, parents, and students. Furthermore, the studies must be carefully designed for the population of students they are conducted on. There have been mixed results of such evaluation studies, but generally the results are positive, indicating that teaching thinking skills is effective in improving people's intellectual competence, at least temporarily and for certain types of problems.

Biological metaphor

Chapter One showed that, according to the biological metaphor, intelligence is defined in terms of biological functions, such as glucose uptake in the brain or electrocortical activity. Improving intelligence as defined by the biological metaphor therefore involves attempting to increase the neurological functioning of a brain region thought to be critical for intellectual functioning (e.g., the frontal lobes, see Chapter One) or perhaps enhancing the efficiency of general neurological processes.

Taking "smart drugs" (also known as nootropics, smart pills, cognitive enhancers, or brain steroids) to enhance memory, attention, or other types of cognitive performance reflects an attempt to improve biological intelligence by influencing the nervous system. It is widely believed, for example, that caffeine enhances mental alertness and that nicotine is associated with increased short-term memory. Recent advances in treating Alzheimer's disease have led to interest in applying similar medical treatments to enhance the intelligence of normally aging people. Such advances involve using drugs to increase the availability of the neurotransmitter acetylcholine, to improve blood flow to the brain, and to enhance the oxygen and glucose uptake in the brain (see Chapter Two). At this time, the evidence indicating an intellectual benefit of using smart drugs is insufficient. True intellectual benefits enjoyed through the use of drugs — if such benefits can be definitively demonstrated — may help us learn about the biological basis of intelligence by revealing how the manipulation of specific neurological processes results in enhancements of intelligent functioning.

The use of drugs does not reflect an attempt to *teach* intelligence, to improve intelligence through instruction. Improving biological intelligence through instruction involves actually teaching people how to enhance the functioning of their own nervous systems. Such an approach to teaching intelligence might involve instruction in biofeedback methods for enhancing electrocortical activity, an approach that has been demonstrated to be somewhat successful in improving the attention levels and IQ scores of children with Attention-Deficit/Hyperactivity Disorder (ADHD) (Fuchs, Birbaumer, Lutzenberger, Gruzelier & Kaiser, 2003; Lubar, Swartwood, Swartwood & O'Donnell, 1995).

For example, in a study conducted by Thomas Fuchs and his colleagues, 22 children diagnosed with ADHD participated in a 12-week program in which they were instructed to increase the activity of certain brain waves and to decrease the activity of others. The children received feedback regarding their success at accomplishing goal-levels of neurological functioning in the style of a computer-game display. Among improvements on other measures (e.g., impulsivity, inattention), there were slight improvements in IQ (three points) as measured by the Wechsler Intelligence Scale for Children-Revised Edition (WISC-R). Though these improvements were small, they were equivalent to improvements made by a comparison group of eleven children who did not engage in biofeedback but received medical treatment for their ADHD. Larger IQ improvements on the WISC-R, an average of approximately nine points, have been found in a sample of 10 children with ADHD who received similar biofeedback training (Lubar, Swartwood, Swartwood & O'Donneu, 1995). Attempts to improve the IQ scores of people without attention disorders, however, have been few and have not had definitive results (Rasey, Lubar, McIntyre, Zoffuto & Abbott, 1996).

The biological metaphor not only provides a target for intelligence instruction (i.e., neurological processes), but it also suggests the optimal timing for intelligence instruction, regardless of the metaphor on which the instruction is based. Many developmental processes in both human and nonhuman animals, such as the development of certain social behaviors, have been found to have an associated biological *critical period*. If an animal does not receive the appropriate stimulation during the critical period, then development does not occur normally despite intervention. That is, even with aid, development after the critical period occurs at a retarded rate or not at all. If there is a critical period for intellectual development, then attempts to improve underdeveloped intelligence are best made during that time.

The idea of a critical period in intellectual development is not a recent one (e.g., see Hunt, 1961; also Garlick, 2002; Grotzer & Perkins, 2000). There have been several attempts that, though not biologically based, were designed to explore the benefits of very early intervention occurring during the supposed critical period. For example, the Carolina Abecedarian Project (see Campbell, Helms, Sparling & Ramey, 1998) began in the early 1970s in part as a response to initial evidence that the effects of Head Start faded over time. A possible explanation for the apparent ineffectiveness of Head Start interventions was that children participated in them *after* the period during which they experienced the most rapid cognitive growth. The Abecedarian Project was designed to target very young children ranging in age from six weeks to six months. Its purpose was to evaluate whether the same intervention could be more effective if delivered at a very early age than if delivered during primary school, when Head Start interventions typically take place. As with most Head Start interventions, the Abecedarian intervention was not based on a particular theory of intelligence, save the belief that modification of intelligence should occur before four years of age.

Other attempts at early intervention include — in addition to the Abecedarian Project — the Milwaukee Project (Garber, 1988) and Project CARE (Wasik, Ramey, Bryant & Spalling, 1990), both of which began at infancy. Together, these three early intervention projects appear to have been successful in increasing the Stanford–Binet IQ scores of three-year-old children, relative to children of the same age who did not participate in the intervention. This advantage was maintained at five years of age, though the difference in IQ points between intervention participants and nonparticipants decreased somewhat. The results from these three projects suggest that there is a critical period for intellectual development — occurring from birth to four years of age — during which attempts to improve underdeveloped intelligence will be more successful than if they are started at a later age (see Ramey, Ramey & Lanzi, 2001). Although some of these projects followed up on their participants after several years, none of the projects involved reassessment of IQ after five years of age. Therefore, the long-term benefit of early intervention could not be assessed. Long-term effects were seen for measures of academic achievement and social adjustment, however.

Instructional interventions stemming from the biological metaphor may prove to be useful for understanding what happens biologically when intelligence develops. By improving certain biological functions through instruction, we may gain insight into how these functions change during the course of unaided development. It can be difficult to demonstrate, however, that maturational processes can be speeded up, as researchers whose attempts to teach intelligence are based on the epistemological metaphor have discovered.

Epistemological metaphor

In order to demonstrate increased intelligence as defined by the epistemological metaphor, children must show that they can advance more quickly through Piaget's stages of cognitive development than their uninstructed peers (see Wagner & Sternberg, 1984). More rapid advancement through these stages would require that instructed children — through accommodation and assimilation — acquire the cognitive structures necessary to perform well on the Piagetian tasks described in Chapter Two more quickly. This means that at a relatively young age instructed children should demonstrate the intellectual capability of children who are much older. Piaget believed that advancement through his stages of intellectual development occurred as a result of biological maturation more than as a function of learning, however. He therefore did not focus on increasing intelligence as defined by his theory, although many psychologists in the United States have.

Early Piagetian training interventions focused primarily on helping preschool children to reach the concrete operations stage more quickly (e.g., Lavatelli, 1970) and on helping adolescents reach the formal operations stage (Lawson, Blake & Nordland 1975). In general, these training programs have sought to develop children's intellectual skills through active, exploratory learning using exercises that are commensurate with the children's developmental levels.

Chapter One explained that children in the concrete operations stage can distinguish objects based on their physical characteristics, such as color, size, or shape, and can also order objects, for example, from smallest to largest. To help preschool children reach the concrete operations stage more quickly, Lavatelli (1970) specified a set of activities to foster the development of the children's ability to classify objects, to understand the fundamental properties of number, measurement, and space, and to arrange objects in some kind of order.

Rejecting the idea that advancement through Piaget's stages be used as a criterion for development, Kamii and DeVries (1977) took a different approach to early education. They supported a broad definition of intellectual capability, which included two major objectives: (1) being able to generate "interesting ideas, problems, and questions," and (2) being able to "put things in relationships and notice similarities and differences" (p. 394). Concordant with Piaget, they believed that independent learning and discovery was the best method for accomplishing intellectual capability.

There have been several attempts to develop formal operations in adolescents (e.g., see Lawson, Blake & Nordland, 1975). These attempts appear to be inspired in part by the fact that approximately 50 percent of adults never reach Piaget's formal operations stage (Kamii & DeVries, 1977; Lawson, Blake & Norland, 1975). It will be remembered from Chapter One that people capable of formal-operational thought exhibit systematic problem-solving skills and approach the world in a scientific way, learning by testing their hypotheses about the world. Anton E. Lawson and his colleagues (Lawson, 1975; Lawson, Blake & Nordland, 1975) sought to develop teaching strategies in the sciences (e.g., biology and physics) that would develop in young adults the ability to think scientifically through problems using a process of exploration, invention, and discovery. In the exploration–invention–discovery learning cycle, students learn how to apply abstract concepts in order to discover the similarities among seemingly diverse events (Lawson, 1975). For example, to understand what makes a scientific experiment "unfair," students in the exploration phase witness several confounded scientific experiments and develop ideas for what makes them inadequate. In the invention phase, students develop a language for discussing what makes the experiments inadequate (i.e., that the variables are not properly controlled). In the discovery phase, students apply the new language to diverse situations in order to see how far the concepts extend.

Evaluation of these early Piagetian programs for increasing intelligence has suggested that Piaget's theory may not be optimally useful for teaching intelligence (Kuhn, 1979). It is unclear, for example, what the rationale is behind speeding up people's movement through Piaget's stages. Moreover, attempts to develop formal operational thought in children and young adults have been largely unsuccessful (see Lawson, Blake & Nordland, 1975), in part because there are problems with how it is determined that the formal operations stage has been reached (Kuhn, 1979). Although none of the early attempts to use Piaget's theory as a model for education have progressed much farther than the experimental stage, more recent interventions have used Piaget-inspired methods to enhance intelligence as measured by other metaphors. One such intervention is that of David P. Weikart and his colleagues, called the Perry Preschool Project, which began in the late 1960s (see Weikart & Schweinhart, 1997).

Similar to Head Start, the Perry Preschool Project was designed to enhance the cognitive and socio-emotional competence of disadvantaged preschool-age children. Consistent with Piaget's thinking, the training provided to children emphasized active and exploratory learning. Moreover, project teachers were instructed to develop scientific thinking in intervention participants through deliberate and systematic help with prediction, observation, explanation, and hypothesis-generation skills. Intellectual benefits reaped by participation in this project were measured using tests of IQ. Children participating in the project showed an increase in IQ relative to nonparticipants in grades three and five, but IQ advantages for program participants at higher grades were not assessed.

The work of Irving E. Sigel and his colleagues represents another Piaget-inspired approach to teaching intelligence (see Sigel, 2002). According to Sigel's Psychological Distancing Model (PDM), children develop the ability to represent thought using language and imagery through a process called *distancing*. In the distancing process, which can be initiated by oneself or by others, children abstract themselves from an immediate experience and take a more reflective stance on what is happening. The representational thinking developed through distancing helps children to learn and acquire knowledge because it makes the processes of assimilating and accommodating new knowledge easier.

Teachers trained on the PDM evoke distancing by asking children to describe an immediate experience, to classify the experience in terms of other experiences, or to evaluate the experience on various dimensions. Sigel evaluated the effectiveness of his distancing model in enhancing the cognitive performance of preschool children from low- and middle-income families and found that children taught to use distancing strategies had better mnemonic, classification, and predictive skills than those children who were not (Sigel & Cocking, 1977; Sigel, Secrist & Forman, 1973).

Because the intelligence theories based on the epistemological metaphor address intellectual development, they seem on the surface to be ideally suited for creating programs to teach intelligence. However, epistemological theories do not actually lend themselves well to teaching intelligence in part because they assume that intellectual development advances as a function of biological maturation and because the validity of stage theories for describing how intelligence develops has been questioned. Instructional interventions based on the sociological metaphor have met with more success.

Sociological metaphor

Understanding how to improve intelligence as defined by the sociological metaphor can be tricky because theories of intelligence based on this metaphor already place an emphasis on the dynamic aspect of cognitive competence. It will be recalled that Vygotsky believed that a child's intelligence could be truly assessed only by examining the difference between what the child can do unassisted and what he can do assisted by a more capable other. Intelligence assessment based on this theory — dynamic testing (see Chapter Two) — already has an instructional component therefore. The key to teaching intelligence according to this metaphor is to expand the upper limits of a child's capability when assisted by a more capable other or, in other words, increase the "width" of her zone of proximal development (Campione, Brown & Ferrara, 1982). This may seem a little counterintuitive, so it is represented in figure 3.1.

In this figure, we see two zones of proximal development, one for a child who has not received instruction and one for a child who has. Both zones of development have the same "starting point" or cognitive task that can be performed without assistance — examining a set of geometric shapes and naming each one. For the child who did not receive instruction, the "outer edge" of her zone of proximal development, or what she can perform with assistance, involves examining a more realistic image (e.g., a picture of a street scene) and identifying the geometric shapes that are present. For the child who did receive instruction, the task that can be performed with assistance involves drawing a realistic image that contains geometric shapes of a certain type, a task that is more difficult than simply recognizing shapes that are present. In other words, a child's zone of proximal development becomes wider when he learns how to effectively transfer "lessons learned" from one kind of problem situation to another. A child whose wider zone of proximal development is depicted in figure 3.1 has learned not just how to recognize geometric shapes in a natural setting, but he can also transfer this knowledge to creating novel objects in natural settings that are composed of geometric shapes.

Vygotsky did not explore methods for enhancing the width of a child's zone of proximal development, although others have with some positive outcomes. One example is Reuven Feuerstein's (1980) Instrumental Enrichment program, which has been successful, in some measure, in Israel (where Feuerstein has worked), and in other parts of the world (though see Blagg, 1991). It is based on Feuerstein's theory of intelligence, and is designed to remedy cognitive deficiencies in both retarded and

Zone of proximal development – no instruction

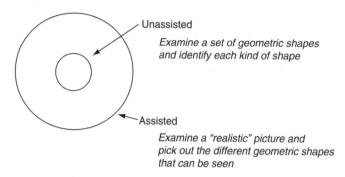

Unassisted

*Examine a set of geometric shapes
and identify each kind of shape*

Assisted

*Examine a "realistic" picture and
pick out the different geometric shapes
that can be seen*

Zone of proximal development – instruction

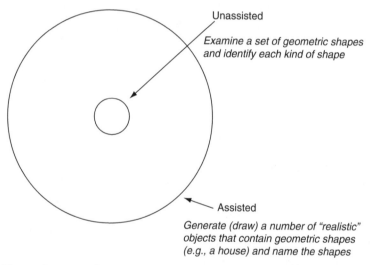

Unassisted

*Examine a set of geometric shapes
and identify each kind of shape*

Assisted

*Generate (draw) a number of "realistic"
objects that contain geometric shapes
(e.g., a house) and name the shapes*

Figure 3.1 *Teaching Intelligence as Defined by the Sociological
Metaphor*

non-retarded children that prevent efficient learning and the
broad application of acquired knowledge and skill. These cognitive deficiencies include: (1) unplanned, impulsive, and unsystematic exploratory behavior, (2) inability to handle multiple
pieces of information simultaneously, and (3) difficulty detecting
and defining problems, among others. By remedying these

deficiencies, children are expected to become better at learning from their experiences and transferring this knowledge or skill from one experience to others. In Vygotsky's terms, such improvements would increase the width of children's zone of proximal development, as they would require fewer hints to acquire new concepts and could apply newly learned concepts to a wider range of problems.

In order to teach these general "learning to learn" skills, Instrumental Enrichment instructors guide children through a set of exercises that involve solving very abstract problems that have no clear connection to the problems found in particular course materials. In fact, the problems in these exercises closely resemble those found on IQ tests. The skills acquired through working on these problems can then be applied to a broad range of more concrete, "realistic" problems with the help of an instructor. For example, in one activity, called "orientation of dots," children practice identifying and outlining sets of geometric figures embedded in a variety of two-dimensional arrays of dots. This exercise is expected to help children focus on information present in a situation and detect meaningful patterns. The Instrumental Enrichment program also involves *bridging*, which is each teacher's effort to help children extend the skills they have learned to concrete, everyday problems. Teachers are instructed to spend at least half their time in bridging activities.

We have already discussed several approaches to teaching "learning to learn" skills, including Binet's mental orthopedics and the training of critical thinking skills, but what distinguishes sociological approaches from other approaches is their emphasis on the social means of communicating what is to be learned and the use of dynamic tests for intelligence assessment. Sociological approaches specifically target a particular set of mental processes and explicitly evaluate their enhancement using dynamic rather than static tests. Anthropological approaches to teaching intelligence also use social contexts for learning, but instead focus on creating cultures that support learning as a lifestyle.

Anthropological metaphor

According to the anthropological metaphor, culture plays a critical role in determining what it means to be intelligent. Culture designates the skills, behaviors, and ways of knowing that are valued by a particular community and that are therefore acquired and passed down from one generation to the next. An important implication of the link between culture and intelligence is that by influencing a particular culture one can influence the intelligence of the members of that culture. Relatively recent research has capitalized on this link by exploring how creating a "community of learning" in the classroom can enhance the intellectual performance of school children (Grotzer & Perkins, 2000).

One of the first people to formally articulate the dispositions of critical thinking and intellectual behavior was John Dewey (1933). Later, philosopher Robert H. Ennis (1987) elaborated on these views. Dewey stressed the importance of such characteristics as open-mindedness, intellectual sensitivity, and focus to reflective thought, which he believed to be critical for intelligent behavior. Ennis listed 14 dispositions that he believed to be essential for critical thinking, which, generally speaking, included desire for information, open-mindedness, precision, focus, and sensitivity to the feelings, knowledge, and sophistication of others. Other researchers have extended Ennis's initial work, further refining the list of critical thinking dispositions and suggesting ways that educators can cultivate them in the classroom by influencing classroom culture (Tishman, Jay & Perkins, 1993). These researchers suggest that educators can foster an intellectual culture by honing students' intellectual capability, raising students' awareness of occasions calling for intelligent behavior, and nurturing students' inclination to behave intelligently (Tishman, Jay & Perkins, 1993).

Several studies have identified cultural norms that, if fostered in the classroom, can positively influence motivation and learning. These norms include group work and orderliness (Bezruczko, Kurland & Eckert, 1996), student autonomy (Deci, Schwartz, Sheinman & Ryan, 1981), and social construction of knowledge (Scardamalia, Bereiter & Lamon, 1994). For example, in one study (Brown & Campione, 1994), researchers compared the reading-comprehension performance of fifth- and sixth-grade children participating in a "community of learners" to that of children taught using reciprocal-teaching techniques and that of children taught in a traditional classroom setting. The community-of-learners children were encouraged to think critically, share their expertise, and discuss course topics with one another in an environment where research, knowledge building, and critical thinking were highly valued. The reciprocal-teaching children led each other in the discussion and learning of class topics. On multiple standardized tests of reading comprehension, the children in the community of learners outperformed students who received the reciprocal-teaching technique, as well as students who received traditional instruction.

Other research has shown that classroom culture can have an effect on how long the positive benefits of intelligence instruction based on other metaphors persist. For example, Bezruczko, Kurland and Eckert (1996) found some relation between, on the one hand, the cultural norms of working together and keeping order and, on the other hand, the length of time that intellectual benefits from Head Start persisted. Although these results are tentative, they may provide some explanation for why the effects of programs like Head Start do not last — that the classroom and home environments children reenter after completing the program may not support intellectual curiosity and continued learning (Evans, 2004; Reynolds, Mavrogenes, Bezruczko & Hagemann, 1996).

The anthropological approach to teaching intelligence has particular promise for helping us to understand how non-ability factors influence the development and continued growth of intelligence. To date, however, instructional interventions taking an anthropological approach to improving intelligence have focused primarily on improving achievement in school, which, for some, serves as a proxy for intelligence (e.g., Binet, [1909]1973). The use of culture to improve how children perform on theory-based intelligence tests has not been as widely studied, though we will present some relevant explorations of this topic in Chapter Five in our discussion of group differences in intelligence.

There remain many additional interesting questions that must be answered in order to fully understand how changes in culture lead to improved intelligence. For example, one open question is whether or not (or how long) the positive intellectual benefits of participating in a particular classroom culture will persist in environments in which a different culture dominates (Grotzer & Perkins, 2000). Another question, of course, is one of what definition of intelligence should be used to guide changes in classroom culture. People who implicitly hold different metaphors for intelligence will have different ideas for what kinds of intellectual capabilities they wish to foster and what kinds of tests will be used to evaluate improvement.

Systems metaphor

Successfully teaching intelligence according to the systems metaphor involves demonstrating an improvement in many areas of intellectual behavior, not just those areas that are typically assessed by standardized tests of intelligence or tests of school achievement. Improvements in school performance are of particular interest to systems theorists, however, because success in school is believed to depend on the functioning of a multifaceted system of intelligence and such success serves as an important gateway to future opportunity. In addition, systems theorists view schools as often failing to reach the many facets of children's intelligence, which makes them an important target for intervention.

Practical Intelligence for School (PIFS)

The PIFS program (Williams, Blythe, White, Li, Sternberg & Gardner, 1996; Williams, Blythe, White, Li, Gardner & Sternberg, 2002) was designed to enhance students' understanding of themselves and the school environment and to help students learn how to use this knowledge to accomplish school-related goals (e.g., achieving a particular grade, getting along with peers). PIFS instruction was delivered via a stand-alone course on self- and task-management skills and also integrated into the core curriculum (English, social studies, science, and math) of the seventh grade. Middle-school students (usually between 10 and 14 years old) were a focus in this intervention because differences in practical intelligence for school begin to appear during the middle-school years and at that time set the stage for future differences in school performance.

PIFS instruction targeted five characteristics thought to be central to students' practical intelligence for school: *knowing why, knowing self, knowing differences, knowing process,* and *revisiting.* Integrated exercises for helping students explore and enhance these five aspects of practical intelligence were coupled with students' regular coursework and applied to the topics of reading and expository writing. For example, in the topic of expository writing, PIFS students are taught to discover why writing is important both in and out of school, to recognize their personal strengths and weaknesses in writing, to distinguish between different styles and strategies of writing, to understand the role of planning and organization in the writing process, and to recognize the importance of revising. Stand-alone exercises were applied homework and testing skills. Students explored, for example, the purposes for homework, personal homework practices, differences in homework requirements for different classes, and strategies for improving the effectiveness of the homework process and homework quality.

Seventh-grade students (usually aged 11–13 years) participating in the PIFS program showed higher scores than nonparticipants on surveys of study habits and attitudes and learning and study skills (Williams, Blythe, White, Li, Sternberg, & Gardner, 1996). PIFS students also outperformed non-PIFS students on academic and practical assessments of reading, writing, homework, and test-taking (Williams, Blythe, White, Li, Gardner & Sternberg, 2002). Together, these results indicate the success of both stand-alone and integrated instruction of practical intelligence, although long-term benefits of the instruction were not assessed.

Building from the successes of the PIFS program, Williams, Sternberg, and colleagues developed an analogous program to PIFS called CIFS (Creative Intelligence for School; Williams, Markle, Brigockas & Sternberg, 2001). In contrast to PIFS, which was designed to help students adapt better to the school environment, CIFS was designed to help middle- and high-school students learn how to adapt the school environment to themselves, fashioning it to their interests and talents through their approach to assignments and projects. It teaches skills and attitudes such as those involved in redefining problems, taking sensible risks, persevering in the face of obstacles, and analyzing one's creative solutions.

Project Spectrum

Project Spectrum began in 1984 as a collaborative effort between David H. Feldman, Howard Gardner, and their colleagues at Harvard and Tufts University. Together, Feldman and Gardner noted that traditional educational curricula failed to nurture the intellectual strengths of many children, who were consequently left behind with often negative effects on their confidence and intellectual development (Feldman, 1998). Project Spectrum used Feldman's and Gardner's theories as a springboard for addressing the failures of traditional education through the assessment and nurturance of children's distinct intellectual strengths.

Feldman's nonuniversal theory (1980) rejected the idea that intelligence develops in the same way in all children despite differences in life experiences and educational access. He instead posited that children's intelligence is gradually developed via accumulated knowledge in the different domains where children acquire experience, such as piano playing or mathematical theorizing. As described in Chapter One, Gardner (1983) rejected the idea that intelligence was a single ability, asserting instead that there are multiple intelligences. Gardner & Feldman used their theories to identify the "spectrum" of young children's intellectual strengths (e.g., see Krechevsky & Gardner, 1990) and to develop a curriculum for nurturing the strengths they identified. With the help of teachers and other outside collaborators, they designed Project Spectrum learning centers in 1990 for at-risk first-graders (aged five to seven years) in Sommerville, Maryland, that would first assess the children's strengths then provide a classroom environment where the children's individual strengths and interests could be nurtured (Chen, Krechevsky, Viens & Isberg, 1998).

Over the course of the year during which the Spectrum learning centers were active, teachers used informal methods to nurture 15 children's strengths and interests, which were later revised into more formal learning activities (Chen, 1998). For instance, teachers provided areas of the classroom where children with particular intellectual strengths could further explore and develop their capabilities. In addition, teachers would inform parents of their child's areas of strength and would ask children to lead activities in these areas. The teachers involved in the program reported that once troubled children were given the opportunity to explore their intellectual strengths, they were transformed, showing enthusiasm and confidence that had not been demonstrated before in the classroom.

In order to affect change in traditional academic subjects, the Project Spectrum team developed what they called a *bridging process*, which was a method for remedying children's intellectual weaknesses in these subjects through calling on their nontraditional intellectual strengths. The bridging process included individual and group techniques to engage the students more fully in learning, including situating the lessons in a realistic activity (e.g., writing letters to friends and relatives to improve writing skills) and using the content of children's strengths to engage them in areas of weakness (e.g., writing an essay about dance to help a child with strength in kinesthetic intelligence remedy her weakness in writing), among others. At the end of the school year, the Sommerville children showed greater engagement in school activities, with individual children showing notable improvements in basic academic skills.

Gardner (1999b) has further described the application of the bridging process to intellectual development. Fundamentally, he seeks to enhance students' ability to understand course materials, that is, to demonstrate an ability to apply learned material to new situations. Gardner outlined three major steps in teaching students to apply learned material to new situations.

The first step is to engage and situate students in the topic to be learned by determining the *entry points* that are best suited to student's intelligences and the course materials. These entry points may be narrational (telling stories), quantitative/numerical (providing numerical information), foundational/existential (presenting "bottom-line" information), aesthetic (using images or works of art), hands-on (facilitating activities), or social (generating discussion and debate). For example, to introduce the topic of the Vietnam War, a teacher could read stories about the war from a soldier's memoir, present numerical information about troops, casualties, and financial costs, discuss what war reveals about human nature, provide photojournalistic images of the war zones, organize a trip to a local Vietnam memorial or exhibit, or facilitate a classroom debate about whether the United States should have become involved in the war.

The second step of the instruction is the telling of analogies. Teachers provide a frame of reference for students by carefully choosing and presenting instructive analogies. For example, to teach about the Vietnam War, a teacher might draw similarities between perceptions of the attempt to prevent the "spread of communism" and efforts to prevent the spread of disease. Students then use this frame of reference as a way of understanding factual material introduced in the third step of instruction. The third and final step of instruction involves presenting course information in depth and from multiple perspectives that call upon student's patterns of intelligences.

Aside from the anecdotes of teachers and researchers involved in Project Spectrum, there currently are no reported data indicating whether the instructional intervention outlined above is effective in developing intellectual competency or if it has long-term effects on children's attitudes towards school (Chen, 1998). Basing classroom instruction on the theory of multiple intelligences is quite popular, however, because of its demonstrated positive effects on children's confidence, motivation, and productivity in the classroom.

Teaching for Successful Intelligence

Similar to Project Spectrum, teaching based on Sternberg's (1988, 1997) triarchic theory of successful intelligence (see Chapter One), targets multiple abilities. In particular, teaching for successful intelligence targets student's analytical, creative, and practical abilities (e.g., see Sternberg & Grigorenko, 2000). The goal of teaching for successful intelligence is to provide students with instruction that allows them to capitalize on their strengths in these abilities but also that challenges them to correct or compensate for their weaknesses. In addition, teaching for successful intelligence is designed to help students develop improved thinking skills, which can be helpful for enhancing all three kinds of ability.

Chapter One stated that analytical abilities are used whenever a person analyzes, evaluates, compares, or contrasts pieces of information. Instruction targeting analytical abilities therefore involves discussions and exercises that emphasize these activities. For example, in a lesson on plant biology, the instructor might ask students to "compare and contrast" the structure of different root systems and "explain" how this structure relates to climate.

It will be recalled that in Chapter One it was also said that creative abilities are involved in the creation, invention, or discovery of objects or ideas. Therefore, instruction targeting creative abilities involves discussions and activities that require students to exercise these abilities. For example, in the plant biology lesson, the instructor might ask students to "suppose that" scientists wanted to grow plants on the moon and "design" a greenhouse that would allow plants to survive in such a hostile climate.

Finally, it was also shown that practical abilities permit people to practice, apply, or use what has been learned in either formal or informal settings. Instruction targeting these abilities therefore involves challenging students to use these skills. In the plant biology lesson, this might involve asking students to "apply" what they have learned about plant's biological systems to growing their own plant or to "demonstrate" how the pruning process increases the number of blooms the plant produces.

Teaching for successful intelligence can be applied to any school topic, and has been evaluated for effectiveness in such topics as psychology (Sternberg, Ferrari, Clinkenbeard & Grigorenko, 1996; Sternberg, Torff & Grigorenko, 1998), reading (Sternberg, Grigorenko & Jarvin, 2001), and social studies (Sternberg, Torff & Grigorenko, 1998) to both gifted students and students not identified as gifted. Working with students in various academic years (i.e., third, fifth [children aged between six and 10 years of age], and eighth grades [12 to 14 years] and high school [13 to 18 years]) Sternberg and his colleagues have found that teaching for successful intelligence improves students' performance on course materials (essays, projects, multiple-choice exams) designed to tap analytical, creative, and practical abilities. It has also been shown to be more effective than standard curricula, which typically are focused primarily on analytical abilities or rote memorization skills. Finally, these researchers found that students who received instruction matching their ability strengths (e.g., creative instruction for children with high creative ability) showed greater improvement than students whose instruction was not matched to their strengths in patterns of ability.

Together, these results suggest that efforts to improve students' analytical, creative, and practical abilities can be successful and that standard curricula could be enhanced through the use of instruction based on the triarchic theory of successful intelligence. Most importantly, students with differing strengths and weaknesses would have equal opportunity to benefit from education. Current research by Sternberg and his colleagues is exploring the effectiveness of teaching for successful intelligence in children aged from four to seven (fourth grade) in reading, science, and mathematics.

Conclusion

In this chapter we have discussed several attempts to improve intelligence via instruction. We began by describing how attempts to increase intelligence differ from educational practices more generally, and by presenting early attempts to improve intelligence that were not based on a particular intelligence theory. Next, we discussed relatively more recent, theory-based attempts to improve intelligence. In general, it appears that teaching intelligence can have immediate benefits on intelligence test performance and on intellectual performance more broadly defined (e.g., school achievement). Most attempts to increase intelligence have not followed up on students after the intervention was conducted, however, so it is unclear how lasting the effects of intelligence instruction are.

We mentioned at the beginning of the chapter that a unifying assumption of attempts to teach intelligence is the belief that intelligence can indeed be taught. It is important to note, however, that many intelligence theorists do *not* believe that intelligence can be changed. Francis Galton, Alfred Binet's contemporary, was one of the first intelligence theorists to put forth the idea that intelligence is inherited genetically and to erroneously believe that if intelligence is genetically inherited that it must be fixed at birth. In the next chapter, we will discuss the exploration of the genetic and environmental origins of intelligence and its controversial findings.

CHAPTER FOUR

The Genetic and Environmental Bases of Intelligence

As we begin our discussion of genes, the environment, and intelligence, we discover that our blind-men-and-the-elephant analogy begins to change shape. Consistent with previous chapters, our blind men would each have different ways of responding to questions about the role of genes in "elephantness." In contrast to previous chapters, the blind men's different ways of responding would come not from their having different definitions of elephantness but from the fact that the genetic basis of elephantness is not of primary interest to some of them. These blind men would have no response to such questions at all, and might even find talk of genes irrelevant and fanciful.

Most of the seven metaphors for conceptualizing intelligence that we have discussed so far are silent with regard to the level of genetic involvement in intelligent behavior. In fact, some metaphors, such as the sociological metaphor and the anthropological metaphor, are fundamentally devoted to exploring non-genetic (i.e., environmental) influences on what it means to be intelligent. Only research characterized by a subset of these seven metaphors — the geographic and, to some extent, biological metaphors — has been explicitly devoted to this subject.

Because we know that intelligence, like all other psychological functions, involves the brain — and the brain is a biological structure just like earlobes and eyes — it is unusual to find scientists who believe that there is absolutely no involvement of genes in intelligent behavior (Dick & Rose, 2002). There linger many misunderstandings, however, regarding what it means to say that differences among people in intelligence can be attributed to heredity (Sternberg & Grigorenko, 1999). In addition, although most scientists recognize some role for genes in intelligence, there is little scientifically known regarding what this role is and how it plays out over time and in different environments.

Attempts to understand the genetic and environmental bases of intelligence have a history replete with many fascinating developments and controversial people and ideas. In this chapter, we present an overview of these developments and the general findings that have resulted from studying genes and intelligence. We also present some interesting new directions that research in this area is just beginning to take at the start of the twenty-first century. In our discussion, we attempt to guide our readers in exploring the key scientific issues surrounding the study of genes, the environment, and intelligence and in interpreting findings regarding the heritability of intelligence. However, we do not suggest any implications of these findings for social policy as others have done (e.g., Goddard, 1919; Herrnstein & Murray, 1994; Rushton & Jensen, in press). Social policy, such as the development of priorities for allocating educational resources or the adoption of eugenic practices, follows from a culture's set of values and is not a topic of this book.

It may have already occurred to the curious reader to wonder why the geographic and biological metaphors, in particular, have been involved in the exploration of the genetic basis of intelligence. Some insight into this curiosity can be achieved by examining the questions that have been pursued in research devoted to this topic.

One of the oldest questions to be asked about genes and intelligence is: *How much can intellectual differences between people be attributed to differences in genetic makeup?* To answer this question, scientists seek to determine why people differ in their intelligence (i.e., because they have different genes ["nature"] or because they came from different environments ["nurture"]) and intelligence is typically defined and tested in accordance with the geographic metaphor (see Chapter Two). Psychologists studying the heritability of intelligence share the fundamental interest of psychologists working with geographic theories of intelligence — people's intellectual differences. Research based on the other metaphors (with the exception of a subset of research based on the computational and biological metaphors — see Chapter One) generally does not have differences among people in intelligence as its primary focus, but rather such topics as the developmental course of intelligence (the epistemological and sociological metaphors), the cultural basis of intelligence (the anthropological metaphor), or some combination of these topics (the systems metaphor).

A second question, more recently asked by researchers studying genetics and intelligence is: *By what mechanisms do genes give rise to intelligent behavior?* To answer this question, scientists seek to identify the genes that are involved in performing on intelligence tests and to determine how these genes influence the development of the neurological structures involved in intelligent functioning. Knowledge about which genes code for intelligent behavior is then applied to understanding why people differ in their intelligence. Exploration of this kind often calls for a link between research exploring intelligence as defined by the biological metaphor and intelligence as defined by the geographic metaphor (Plomin, 2002). The relatively recent efforts to understand the genetic basis of intelligence have benefited from advances in the science and technology of genetics not available until quite recently. They represent a substantial advancement in our understanding of the genetic basis of intelligence during the relatively short time that has followed the pioneering explorations conducted in the mid-late 1800s.

Early Research — "Nature vs. Nurture"

Francis Galton, the first scientist to explore the relative effects of genes and environment on intelligent behavior, is credited with starting the "nature versus nurture" debate over the origins of intellectual differences between people (Plomin, DeFries & McClearn, 1990). Deeply inspired by the theory of evolution put forth by his cousin, Charles Darwin, Galton sought to determine the degree to which intelligence is genetically inherited (Galton, 1869). His interest in this subject preceded the development of intelligence tests (though see Chapter Two for Galton's role in intelligence-test development), so he relied on what he called "eminence" as an indicator of a man's intellectual competency (Galton did not study women). Galton assigned eminence to scholars, military commanders, artists, politicians, and religious leaders, among others, through careful review of biographies and other public records, and by conducting interviews. A man earned the designation "eminent" if he demonstrated consistent intellectual and creative leadership, and if he was recognized by his peers and successors as someone responsible for genuine societal development. Only one in 4,000 men could earn this designation, and Galton identified 1,000 such men.

Galton then studied the pedigrees of these men, discovering that a relatively small number of families produced a relatively large number of eminent men. In other words, the incidence of eminent men in this small group of families was much greater than the overall incidence of one in 4,000, suggesting that familial membership played an important role in determining eminence. Galton further discovered that a man in these families was more likely to be eminent himself the more closely he was related to an eminent man. That is, a man was more likely to be eminent if his father was eminent than if his uncle was eminent. Sons of eminent men were more likely to be eminent than grandsons.

Searching for possible environmental (i.e., non-genetic) explanations for his findings, Galton also explored the backgrounds of his eminent men, finding that some of them came from humble beginnings. Further, he found that boys adopted by eminent fathers and raised in privilege were less likely to be eminent than the natural-born, privileged sons of eminent men. Finally, Galton found that the incidence of eminent men in the United States was no greater than that found in his home country of England despite greater opportunity for social mobility in the United States. Galton's conclusions from this evidence – that intelligence was entirely genetically determined and therefore a capacity in individuals that was fixed at birth – launched the nature–nurture debate.

Galton's conclusions were, in retrospect, a bit hasty and, in fact, wrong, but current scientific methodology and knowledge regarding genes and intelligence owes a great deal to his early work and that of his intellectual successors. Because of his interest in the joint influence of genes and environment on intellectual capacity, Galton is considered the originator of *behavior genetics*, which is a field of study devoted to understanding the interactive effects of genes and environment on various kinds of behavior, including intelligence and personality. A tremendous amount of effort since Galton's time has been devoted to developing sophisticated methods for teasing apart genetic and environmental influences on people's intellectual differences. Modern behavior geneticists attempt to determine the relative importance of genes and environment using these methods, rather than trying to pit one factor against the other in a winner-take-all battle as Galton did.

Methods Used in Behavior—Genetic Research

Following the early work of Galton, studies of the heritability of intelligence have led to developments in research methodologies that scientists believe allow them to control better one factor (genes or environment) while examining the effects of variability in the other factor. To get a better understanding of the information these methodologies are designed to provide, imagine an experimenter who wants to explore the relative effects of plant type and watering on plant growth. How would he or she determine which of these two factors, plant type or watering, is more important in determining the height that plants achieve?

One way is to water in different amounts several plants of the same type. If the plants achieve different heights as a function of the how much water they received, the experimenter would conclude that amount of water is more important than plant type. Alternatively, the experimenter could give the same amount of water to several plants of different types. If the plants achieve different heights—and plants of similar types are more alike in height than plants of more varied types—then height in this situation would appear to be due more to plant type than to watering. When studying differences in human intelligence, people's "type" is their genetic makeup, and the "amount of water" they receive is the environmental conditions in which they develop intellectually.

Of course, conducting experiments that are analogous to the one above would be unethical. They would involve, for example, intentionally placing children in environments of differing qualities to see if genes can make up the difference, or cloning the same person lots of times to explore the effects of different environments. Therefore, the methodologies that we describe below take advantage of natural occurrences when genetically related people grow up in different environments and vice versa. We first describe the methods, and then we discuss the general findings about the heritability of intelligence that are derived from them.

Family studies

The assumption underlying family studies is that if a particular characteristic is influenced by genetics, then people who are more similar genetically will be more similar with regard to that characteristic than people who are less genetically similar. Our current knowledge about genetics allows us to rank pairs of family members in the following manner according to their average degree of genetic similarity (from greatest to least similarity): (1) identical (monozygotic) twins, (2a) fraternal (dizygotic) twins, (2b) full siblings, (3) parent–offspring, and (4) half siblings. The intellectual similarity among these different types of familial relation can be determined by administering a test of intelligence to pairs of individuals from many families and computing the correlation between the test scores. Higher test-score correlations indicate greater intellectual similarity. If test-score correlations among pairs of individuals who share more genes are higher than those among pairs of individuals who share fewer genes, one would consider this evidence that intelligence is influenced by genes.

Family studies date back to the late 1920s, but early family studies generally involved small samples of participants and were not well standardized in their methodology (Grigorenko, 2000), precluding conclusions regarding the intellectual similarity of people with differing degrees of relatedness. A relatively more recent family study, conducted in Hawaii (DeFries, Johnson, Kuse, et al. 1979), was much larger, involving 1,816 families and 15 tests of various intellectual abilities. This study unfortunately did not report varying family relationships, such as parent–offspring, grandparent–grandchild, aunt/uncle–niece/nephew, half sibling–full sibling, however. Therefore the relative intellectual similarity of people with varying genetic relatedness could not be evaluated. Perhaps because of the difficulty and expense involved in conducting them, family studies have not contributed the majority of the data to our understanding of the heritability of intelligence.

An important limitation of family studies is that it can often be quite difficult, if not impossible, to tease genetic effects apart from non-genetic effects. For example, family studies examining the relation between parents and offspring often involve administering intelligence tests to the parents that are different from those administered to the offspring (Bouchard & McGue, 1981). Because intelligence tests are not exactly alike, giving parents and offspring two different tests can result in an under-estimation of intellectual similarity. Consider also the comparison between half siblings and full siblings, who are expected, on the basis of genetics, to have different degrees of intellectual similarity (full siblings more, half siblings less). Because half siblings may differ substantially in their initial home environments while full siblings presumably do not, it is impossible to attribute the lesser degree of intellectual similarity among half siblings relative to full siblings definitively to genes or environment.

Twin studies

One concrete example of Galton's contribution to current behav-ior–genetic methodology was his introduction of the use of twins to explore the question of nature versus nurture (Galton, 1876). Although the method used in twin studies today did not origin-ate with Galton (Rende, Plomin & Vandenberg, 1990), he was the first to make use of the genetic similarity among twins in an attempt to explore the impact of genes and environment on intelligent behavior. Specifically, he studied whether "dissimi-lar" (non-identical) twins became more similar over time despite different environments, which he believed would indicate a dominant effect of genes. He also explored whether "similar" (physically alike, but not necessarily monozygotic) twins became more different over time despite similar genes, which would indicate a dominant effect of environment.

Although other researchers succeeding Galton worked with twins (e.g., Thorndike, 1905), refinement of twin studies following Galton's early work did not occur until the 1920s, after a brief hiatus in twin research. By this time, a clear bio-logical distinction had been made between monozygotic twins and dizygotic twins, a distinction that American psychologist Curtis Merriman and German dermatologist Hermann Siemens noted was useful for understanding the genetic inheritance of characteristics (Rende, Plomin & Vandenberg, 1990). Specifically, they noted that because the degree of genetic similarity among monozygotic ("one-egg") twins was greater than that of dizygotic ("two-egg") twins, then monozygotic twins should resemble each other more on various inherited characteristics than should dizygotic twins. Previous to this time, there had been some confusion as to the relative genetic similarity of "similar" and "dissimilar" twins, with some arguing that there was no distinction to be made between different kinds of twins (Thorndike, 1905).

Twin studies that compare the intellectual similarity of monozygotic twins relative to dizygotic twins have become a hallmark of much modern behavior–genetic research. If intelligence is genetically based, then the correlation of intelligence-test scores between pairs of monozygotic twins, who are genetically identical, will be greater than that between pairs of dizygotic twins who share, on average, only 50 percent of their genes. The assumption behind comparing monozygotic and dizygotic twins is that the two types of twin do not differ in terms of how similar their childhood environments are. For this reason, twin studies are believed to have an advantage over family studies because the similarity-of-environment assumption cannot be made when comparing half siblings to, say, full siblings. The childhood environment that half siblings share is likely more different from each other than the childhood environment that full siblings share because, for example, half siblings only share one parent, but full siblings share both parents. The childhood environments shared by monozygotic twins are assumed to be as different from each other as are the childhood environments shared by dizygotic twins because both types of twin share both parents.

The similarity-of-environment assumption has been challenged, however, by those who suggest that because monozygotic twins look identical, they will be treated more similarly than dizygotic twins, who can appear quite different (Mandler, 2001). This greater similarity in treatment, and therefore similarity in life experiences, would constitute a more similar environment, which could result in greater similarity in intelligence. The concern is that if greater intellectual similarity among monozygotic twins was attributed to genes alone, genes would get too much of the credit, so to speak. Although it has been shown that identical twins are often treated more similarly than fraternal twins (see Mandler, 2001), it remains an open question as to whether these differences in treatment have an effect on intellectual behavior.

An especially powerful kind of twin study involves comparing the intellectual similarity of monozygotic twins who are reared apart relative to monozygotic twins reared in the same home. The hypothesis is that if identical twins growing up in the same home are just as alike in their intelligence as identical twins reared apart, then differences in environment had little impact on intelligence (i.e., genes are the primary reason that people differ in their intelligence). This kind of study assumes that twins reared in different homes grow up in different environments, another assumption that has been challenged (Mandler, 2001). Because ethics prevent researchers (and adoption agencies) from having one twin placed in a good home and the other placed in a bad home, it can be difficult to examine the effects of environments that are truly very different.

Some of the earliest and best known twins-reared-apart studies were conducted by British psychologist Cyril Burt in the mid 1950s (Burt, 1955, 1958, 1966). Burt found in repeated studies that monozygotic twins reared together showed an almost perfect correlation with each other on various tests of intellectual ability. Moreover, he found that monozygotic twins reared apart showed only slightly less intellectual resemblance, even though their family environments differed. Burt used these and related data to argue that relative to genetics, the environment played no real role in why people differed in their intelligence and accomplishments.

Closer examination of Burt's data has revealed, however, that Burt was astonishingly careless and probably deliberately misleading in the reporting of his data—to the point that his numbers cannot be trusted (see Mackintosh, 1995a). Burt's roguish behavior should not be used to discredit the pursuit of understanding the genetic basis of intelligence, but it should be considered sufficient reason to avoid using Burt's findings when reviewing the literature on this topic, as most have done (e.g., Bouchard & McGue, 1981; see also Mackintosh, 1995a). Interestingly, twin studies following Burt's work generally support his findings that monozygotic twins reared apart have notable intellectual resemblance, though not quite to the same degree as suggested in his studies (Mackintosh, 1995b; Scarr & Carter-Saltzman, 1982).

A final kind of twin study is called the *families-of-identical-twins* method, in which the offspring of monozygotic twins are studied. Imagine that we studied several pairs of female identical twins in which both women married and had children. In this unusual situation, the children of these women are equally genetically related to their aunt (sharing 50 percent of her genes) as they are to their mother because the two women are genetically identical. This genetic similarity allows for some interesting investigation of environmental effects on intelligence because offspring of the "same" (genetically speaking) parent are raised in different households. This method is not frequently used, however, because it is not as powerful as other twin methods (Plomin, DeFries & McClearn, 1990).

Adoption studies

In adoption studies, researchers examine the intellectual similarity between parents and their adopted children compared to the intellectual similarity between the same parents and their biological children. Intellectual resemblance between biological siblings and adopted siblings is also compared. The general hypothesis is that if intelligence is heritable, then people who are biologically related will be more intellectually similar than people who are not biologically related. More specifically, biological siblings will be more similar intellectually than non-biological siblings. In addition, offspring will be more intellectually similar to their biological parents than adopted children are similar to their adopted parents.

Adoption studies date back to the late 1920s and 1930s, with the work of such pioneers as Barbara Burks (1928), Alice M. Leahy (1935), and Marie Skodak and Harold Skeels (1949). Together, these researchers examined over 800 families across the continental United States and found, in general, that the expectation of greater intellectual similarity among people who are biologically related was borne out by the data. Relatively more recent large adoption studies include the Texas Adoption Project (Horn, Loehlin & Willerman, 1979), The Minnesota Transracial Adoption Study (Scarr & Weinberg, 1976), and The Adolescent Adoption Study (Scarr & Weinberg, 1978; Scarr & Yee, 1980). These studies also revealed greater intellectual similarity among biologically related people than among non-biologically related people.

Calculating the Effects of Nature and Nurture

Each of the methodologies we described above—family studies, twin studies, and adoption studies—produces what is called a *heritability estimate*, which is an estimate of the degree to which the dissimilarity among people on a particular characteristic is due to genetic inheritance. Theoretically, it ranges from zero, indicating no heritability, to one, indicating complete heritability.

A heritability estimate of zero occurs when all of the variation between people in a particular characteristic is due to environmental influence. This might occur, for example, if there was no variation in genes among these people but substantial variation in the environmental properties they have experienced that are relevant to the characteristic of interest. One hundred percent of the differences observed among these people would be due to the influence of these characteristic-relevant environmental properties.

A heritability estimate of one occurs when all of the variation between people in a particular characteristic is due to genetic influence. This might occur, for example, if everyone in a particular group of people has experienced the exact same characteristic-relevant environmental properties up to the time the estimate was made, but is different genetically. One hundred percent of the differences observed among these people would be due to the variation in their genes, because the characteristic-relevant properties of the environments in which they grew up were identical.

Presumably, if the members of a group of people are genetically identical and they have experienced identical characteristic-relevant environmental properties, then there is no dissimilarity among them on the characteristic of interest! Heritability estimates of zero and one do not occur for intellectual characteristics. They represent theoretical values, rather than actual ones. As a more realistic example, if the heritability of intelligence were determined to be 0.25 in a particular group of people, then dissimilarity among these people would be reduced by 25 percent if they were genetically identical. By extension, dissimilarity in intelligence in this same group would be reduced by 75 percent if non-genetic factors relevant to intellectual development were completely controlled.

There are many things that a heritability estimate for intelligence does *not* indicate (Sternberg & Grigorenko, 1999). First, the heritability estimate does not indicate the proportion of an individual person's intelligence that is "due" to his genes, or how much his intelligence would increase or decrease if he had different genes. Heritability estimates are intended to provide a means for determining the relative importance of genetic and non-genetic factors in understanding why people differ in a particular *population*. They are not designed to provide insight into where a particular person's intelligence "comes from." For this reason, heritability is called a population characteristic, because it refers to an entire population and not to individuals within that population.

Second, a heritability estimate does not indicate the presence of a fixed intellectual capacity. Put another way, the presence of a genetic influence on intelligence does not indicate that people's levels of intelligence are predetermined and unmodifiable. In fact, the heritability and the modifiability of intelligence are unrelated. Consider, for example, height. Height is a highly heritable characteristic (i.e., differences among people in height frequently appear to be largely due to genetic differences), but height can be reduced through environmental stressors, such as prenatal exposure to toxins and childhood malnutrition, or enhanced through medical interventions, such as the injection of growth hormones. In addition, average height has increased dramatically and rapidly throughout the past several generations, as has IQ (Flynn, 1987; Sternberg & Grigorenko, 1999).

Finally, the heritability estimate does not provide an overall, "final" answer on the relative contribution of genes versus the environment to intelligent behavior. The heritability estimate indicates the relative influence of genetics and environment for a particular group of people at a particular time. It is *only* applicable to that particular group of people at that particular time. Consider, for example, the relative size of the heritability estimate for intelligence in two different hypothetical countries. In the first country, the people studied each came from widely different environments (e.g., some educated in private schools and raised in supportive homes, some raised in abusive homes and never receiving an education). In the second country, the people studied each came from quite similar environments. In the first country, the heritability estimate, indicating the role of genetic factors, would be smaller than in the second country, simply because there was greater variability in the environment in the first country than in the second one. The effect of making previously diverse environments in the same country more similar, such as through even redistribution of wealth and opportunity, would be to increase heritability in the same country over time.

Summary of Results — Which is More Important: Nature or Nurture?

The methods that we have described above have been used in numerous studies sampling tens of thousands of biological family members, non-biological family members, and twins, largely from white, middle-class families in North America and Europe (e.g., see Bouchard & McGue, 1981; Grigorenko, 2000). Overall, it has been found that genetic similarity among white middle-class family members appears to go hand-in-hand with intellectual similarity (Grigorenko, 2000). Monozygotic twins, who are genetically the most similar of all possible couplings (excepting clones), have the most similar intelligence test scores. Likewise, full siblings are more similar in their intelligence than half siblings. Parents and their offspring show less intellectual similarity than full siblings, but more than half siblings. Furthermore, studies using different methods for estimating heritability (twin studies, adoption studies, etc.) seem to converge on heritability estimates between 0.50–0.70 for preadolescents and young adults (Grigorenko, 2000) and around 0.75 for adults over the age of 20 years (McGue, Bouchard, Iacono & Lykken, 1993; McGue & Christensen, 2001, 2002). On the basis of these findings — keeping in mind their applicability only to white middle-class families — it is generally concluded that genetics play an important role in intelligence.

Although this conclusion seems to threaten the importance of environmental contributions to intelligence, it is actually a very different conclusion than that originally drawn by Galton — that nature dominates over nurture and intellectual capacity is fixed at birth. Increased knowledge about genetic mechanisms has created awareness that genes are not destiny. We know that genes and environment work together from conception onward to create the variation we see in intelligence and many other traits (Dick & Rose, 2002), so their segregation into separate influences is misguided. In other words, the answer to the question of why people differ in their intelligence is not "nature" or "nurture," but "both!"

As scientific knowledge about genetics develops — and concerns about the validity of methods used to estimate heritability mount — many scientists have begun to question the utility of continuing to ask questions about nature and nurture (e.g., Block, 1995; Grigorenko, 2000). Although 150 years of asking this question have led to the acceptance that genes play an important role in intelligence, they have not illuminated *how* genes and environment interact to influence intelligent behavior. More recent trends in behavior–genetic research, which we will describe below, reflect waning interest in the nature–nurture debate and increased enthusiasm for determining the genetic mechanisms through which genes and environments work jointly to result in intelligent behavior.

Genetic Mechanisms and Intelligence

Brief overview of genetic mechanisms

We begin our discussion with a (very) brief primer on genetics, a field whose origins date back to the late 1800s, because a basic understanding of the purpose that genes serve — creating and maintaining variability in a population — helps us to understand the kinds of questions that behavior–genetic researchers ask about genetics and intelligence and the methods they use for finding answers. Such a discussion naturally starts with Charles Darwin, who was the first to note the tremendous variability among living things while providing a formal attempt to account for the origins and mechanisms of that variability.

Variety, Evolution, and Genetic Inheritance

Darwin ([1859] 1999) argued in his book, *The Origin of Species*, that variety truly is the "spice of life." Or, at least, the "spice of evolution." He asserted that the present form of a species evolved from some previous form, and that variability within a species—acted on by natural selection—makes this evolution, this slow change in the design of a species, possible.

Consider the simplified, fictitious example of a species of fish in which there is some variability in the size of the fish's tailfins and that larger tailfins allow the fish possessing them to swim faster. Now imagine that this species of fish is exposed to predators that can swim quite rapidly. Provided that only fish with larger tailfins can outswim their predators and survive to maturity, only larger tailfins will be passed on to future generations. This would have the overall effect of allowing the species of fish to evolve into one with generally larger (as large as they need to be to outswim predators), but still variable, tailfin sizes. If all of the fish in the species had the exact same size tailfin, and it was too small to allow them to outswim predators, then all of the fish would become victims and the species would come to an end. It is their initial variability that allowed them to change, adapt, and survive.

Darwin believed that the essential variety among members of a species was somehow passed on from parent to offspring, but he did not know how. Using our example above, what allows the offspring of a large-tailfin fish to have, on average, a large tailfin and the offspring of small-tailfin fish to have, on average, a small tailfin? For Darwin, the answers to such questions were not forthcoming.

The earliest published work that could correctly address this issue was that of Darwin's contemporary, Gregor Mendel ([1865] 1967), an Augustinian monk who studied the effects of cross-breeding pea plants with differing characteristics. Darwin and many others overlooked Mendel's work, and it was not until 1900 that it had an influence on scientific thinking about heredity (see Plomin, DeFries & McClearn, 1990). Mendel's three laws for the inheritance of a characteristic, now commonly studied in high school biology courses, set the stage for an explosion in genetic research and the eventual "cracking" of the genetic code that gives rise to all forms of life.

Mendel posited that a pea plant's characteristics, such as the roundness or color of its seeds, were passed on to its offspring via "elements" of heredity. He hypothesized that for each characteristic, two parent plants each contributed one element to an offspring plant and that the combination of these two elements in the offspring resulted in a particular observed characteristic in the offspring. The offspring, in turn, would pass on one of its two elements for each characteristic to its offspring. By positing these elements, Mendel could accurately predict what the offspring of certain combinations of pea plants would look like.

Consider what happened when Mendel bred one plant that always produced round seeds (when self-pollinated or crossed with the same kind of plant) with a plant that always produced wrinkled seeds (when self-pollinated or crossed with the same kind of plant). Mendel found that this combination of "true-breeding" plants always resulted in offspring that produced round seeds. Mendel hypothesized that each truebreeding parent plant contained two identical versions of the elements of heredity, such that a round-truebreeding plant had two "round-seed elements" (e.g., $S_r S_r$) and a wrinkled-truebreeding plant had two "wrinkled-seed elements" (e.g., $S_w S_w$). Each parent plant then passed one of their elements to their offspring, such that all of the offspring had two different (i.e., $S_r S_w$) elements of heredity with regard to seed roundness. Mendel hypothesized that one element dominated over the other—in this case S_r dominated over S_w—and that the offspring plants' observed characteristics reflected this dominance.

Mendel's laws could also explain the outcome of breeding two hybrid pea plants, that is, two plants that each possess one round-seed element, S_r, and one wrinkled-seed element, S_w. Each hybrid parent plant had a 50 percent chance of passing on one or the other of its elements for a particular characteristic to its offspring such that, on average, it would pass on the element, S_r, to two of four offspring and element, S_w, to the other two of four offspring. The four offspring resulting from the cross of two hybrid plants, then, would have the following elemental makeup:

$$1 \text{ plant} = S_r S_r; \quad 2 \text{ plants} = S_r S_w; \quad 1 \text{ plant} = S_w S_w.$$

Here, too, Mendel's hypothesized dominance would affect the observed characteristics of his plants. Three of the four plants would produce round seeds because they contain at least one dominant S_r element. One of the four plants would produce wrinkled seeds because it contains two recessive S_w elements.

We now call Mendel's elements of heredity *genes*, more specifically alternate forms of genes, called *alleles*, which are located on the chromosomes in every cell nucleus. Genes are strips of DNA that code for a particular chain of amino acid molecules, which serve as the building blocks for protein. Proteins, in turn, serve as the building blocks of living things. Genes also control the activation and de-activation of other genes. The correct functioning of genes is critical for the normal development not only of human beings, but of all living things.

Humans have somewhere between 30,000 and 40,000 genes, which together create a tremendous variety of proteins (Plomin, 2002), but just how proteins result in particular observed characteristics or behaviors is unknown. We do know, however, that the link between genes and behavior is indirect and is mediated by such physiological structures as the nervous system. That is, proteins created by genes somehow affect the development of the spinal cord and brain, which in turn plays a role in behavior. As described in Chapter One, much of the brain's role in behavior is yet unknown.

Two Kinds of Variety: Single-Gene and Polygenic Characteristics

The leap between Mendel's pea plants and human intelligence can seem pretty staggering. After all, how does knowing that genes affect whether a pea plant's seeds are round or wrinkled help us understand how genes affect whether someone's IQ is 95 or 125? The leap becomes a little bit less considerable when we understand that characteristics can vary for two different reasons. The variability in a characteristic, such as those Mendel studied, can be influenced by a single gene, or the variability can be influenced by multiple genes, such as intelligence often is. Variability in characteristics influenced by a single-gene has an either–or nature in that variety stems from organisms exhibiting either one version of a characteristic or another (e.g., round seeds or wrinkled seeds). Variability in characteristics influenced by multiple genes has a continuous nature in that variety stems from organisms exhibiting the characteristic to a lesser or greater degree (e.g., higher or lower IQ score).

The genetic inheritance of characteristics influenced by multiple genes, or *polygenic characteristics*, occurs in the same fashion as characteristics influenced by single genes, or *single-gene characteristics*. That is, parents each pass one allele of each gene on to their offspring. A key difference is that in the single-gene case, only one gene is implicated in the appearance of a particular characteristic, whereas in the polygenic case, multiple genes are implicated in the relative degree to which a particular characteristic is displayed. As an analogy, when one flips a single coin one time, one can get either a head or a tail, but when one flips multiple coins 100 times, one can get anywhere from zero heads to 100 heads (although either of these two extremes is highly unlikely). The total number of heads depends on the outcome of each the 100 coin flips. If each person's polygenic characteristics were made up of, say, 100 "coin flips" (i.e., genes), the range in possible levels of these characteristics could be quite wide. When one considers that many genes have more than two alleles (i.e., there are more than two sides to the coin), the possible variety in both single-gene and polygenic characteristics becomes astounding.

At this point, our discussion turns to intelligence. We have argued that genes are the mechanism through which variation passes from one generation to the next and that genes can influence various characteristics either alone or in concert with other genes. As researchers have explored the genetic mechanisms for variety in intelligence, they have found both single-gene effects and polygenic effects on intelligence, and that slightly different genetic mechanisms result in below-normal intelligence or retardation and in normal variation in intelligence (see e.g., Grigorenko, 2000).

Genes and below-normal intelligence

Single-Gene Effects

As our readers might have guessed, it is less difficult to detect the relatively large effects of single genes on intelligence than it is to detect the relatively small effects of multiple genes. Single-gene effects, though less complicated than polygenic effects, can still have profound implications for intelligent functioning. One such single-gene effect is that of the gene that creates or activates a particular enzyme called phenylalanine hydroxylase, which converts an amino acid, called phenylalanine, into tyrosine, an important substance for physical functioning.

As the preceding discussion of Mendel's pea plants stated, genes come in multiple versions, called alleles. Some of these versions are dominant over other versions, which are called recessive. Like the recessive allele of the gene for seed shape (S_w), there is a mutated recessive allele of the gene for the phenylalanine hydroxylase enzyme that prevents the enzyme from being produced or activated. If a person possesses two copies of this mutated allele (one from each parent), then phenylalanine—which enters the body through the consumption of a wide variety of foods—cannot be converted into tyrosine and a disease called *Fölling's disease*, or *phenylketonuria* (PKU), results.

As mentioned above, people with PKU are unable to metabolize the amino acid called phenylalanine, which enters the body through the consumption of a wide variety of foods. The inability of people with Fölling's disease to metabolize phenylalanine results in the build up of phenylpyruvic acid in the urine and in the suppression of other amino acids that are critical for providing nutrition to the nervous system. Deprived of this nutrition, the nervous system cannot function properly, and mental retardation, among other symptoms, often results.

Having the gene for PKU, however, does not necessarily mean a person will be unable to function normally. In the years since Asbjörn Fölling first discovered the disease in 1934, several attempts have been made to treat it or to prevent its effects from occurring. It has been determined that providing infants who have the PKU gene with a low-phenylalanine diet from birth onward appears to have beneficial effects for alleviating the symptoms of the disease, including intellectual benefits (Plomin, DeFries & McClearn, 1990).

The successful screening and treatment of PKU patients indicates the important effects that the environment can have on the expression of genes. Although intervention does not work for all people, and some people with the gene do not exhibit retardation, the overall positive effect of environmental intervention for PKU patients is an excellent case against the idea that genes are "destiny." Despite the widely acknowledged importance of environments in the expression of genes and the demonstration of intelligence, however, there is much to be learned about which environments are important and when they are most likely to have their effects (Mandler, 2001).

We saw in the above example what can possibly happen when just a single gene results in the dysfunction of just a single enzyme. In order to truly understand the effects of multiple genes and intelligence, we need to understand not simply what enzymes correspond to what genes but also how the functioning of multiple enzymes results in intellectual functioning. Much of the knowledge that we need is as yet unavailable, though there are a number of genetic anomalies that have been linked to below-normal intelligence.

Polygenic Effects

Although much is unknown about the mechanisms through which multiple genes influence physical characteristics and behavior, it is readily observable that genetic anomalies can have severe consequences and important implications for intelligent behavior. Abnormalities in the chromosomes, which carry genes, affect many genes at once and frequently result in mental retardation.

One commonly known chromosomal abnormality is *Down's syndrome*. Down's syndrome results from the presence of an extra chromosome 21, and produces a wide range of abnormalities, including a wide space between the first two toes, additional neck tissue, muscle weakness, and slanted eyes, among others. The average IQ of people with Down's syndrome is less than 50, which is 20 points below the cut off for mental retardation. Approximately 95 percent of people with Down's syndrome have an IQ between 20 and 80. People with Down's syndrome constitute approximately 10 percent of the population of the institutionalized mentally retarded, making Down's syndrome the single most important cause of mental retardation (Plomin, DeFries & McClearn, 1990).

Another important chromosomal anomaly affecting intelligence is the presence of extra X chromosomes in either women (called Triple-X females) or men (who have Klinefelter's syndrome). Approximately 75 percent of females with one extra X chromosome display learning problems. Approximately 25 percent of males with one extra X chromosome have below-normal IQs and also demonstrate a delay in language acquisition. People with more than one extra X chromosome experience even more severe intellectual deficits.

Although we have learned a great deal about genetic links to below-normal intelligence, a somewhat different question is posed when exploring the genetic basis of normal variation in intelligence. Differences among people falling within the average range of IQ scores are much more subtle and much more common than differences between people having normal and people having below-normal IQ scores. In addition, differences in normal intelligence are not as easily linked to genes and are not at all linked to the genes associated with mental retardation (Grigorenko, 2000).

Genes and normal variation in intelligence

The exploration of the genetic basis of normal variation in intelligence involves the application of modern molecular–genetic techniques to answering the long-asked questions about why people differ in their intelligence (Plomin, 2002). That is, the questions asked about the genetic basis of intelligence still involve exploring why people differ in their intelligence, but molecular-genetic methods are used in an attempt to answer these questions, rather than statistical methods, such as the heritability estimate.

Single-Gene Effects

Imagine what it would mean for there to be a single gene that causes normal variation in intelligent behavior. Based on what we have learned about Mendel's work and the mechanisms of genetic inheritance, we would have to conclude that a single gene for intelligence would mean that there is one amino acid, one protein, and one overall effect on the structuring of the nervous system. The result would be that normal variation in intelligence would simply involve people who are retarded and people who are of normal intelligence.

Clearly this is not what we see. We see a wide range of intelligence in the people around us, from those who are mentally retarded to those who are among the gifted and talented. This wide range in intellectual capability flatly refutes the idea that there is a single "intelligence gene." Scientists studying the genetic basis of intelligence have long agreed that there must be multiple genes that contribute to intellectual competency. However, just how many genes make this contribution, and how much contribution they make, is still an open question.

Polygenic Effects

Procedures for identifying the multiple genes involved in normal variation in intelligence have their origins in genetic research done in the 1980s. This work resulted in the development of a method that allows researchers to examine particular fragments of DNA called *genetic markers*. To create markers, special enzymes are used to "cut" particular sequences of nucleotide bases that make up DNA. To study intelligence, researchers use markers that surround genes that are believed to be related to neurological functioning. Such genes might be those that result in the development and functioning of neurotransmitter receptors in the brain. When markers on each side of a gene are found, they can be isolated and cloned so that scientists can study the process through which the gene acts (i.e., what amino acid it codes, how this amino acid results in proteins and enzymes, and what physiological structures are affected by the process).

Different people have different lengths of DNA fragments, which are captured by these markers. An important implication of this difference in DNA-fragment length is that researchers can now examine differences among people in DNA itself, rather than in the products of particular genes, such as phenylalanine metabolism in our PKU example. Particular alleles captured by markers can be identified and their relative frequency in different samples of people (e.g., high IQ and low IQ) can be determined. If there are different frequencies found in different samples, then the allele is believed to be important for the characteristic that differentiates the two groups (e.g., intelligence). Within the first few years of the twenty-first century, particular alleles involved in intelligence have not been consistently identified and progress in this research, though exciting, as been slower than expected (Plomin, 2002).

One possible reason for this slow progress is that, by the beginning of 2004, only three major categories of genetic markers have been developed, and they do not capture all of the variation in DNA that exists among people. In order to capture this variation, the entire sequence of the more than three billion nucleotide base pairs in the DNA double helix would have to be determined. No small task! In addition, it is possible that when multiple genes influence a single characteristic there may be many genes with only very small effects, which the technology has difficulty detecting.

Summary

The study of the genetic basis of intelligence has been controversial since its inception. One source of this controversy is the tremendous amount of societal value placed on intellectual competency combined with the mistaken assumption that heredity equals destiny. Another stems from disagreement over how intelligence is conceptualized and measured. A very important source of this controversy is concern that past findings about heritability have been used as a justification for such unethical and immoral practices as slavery and the eugenics movement founded by Galton, which was adopted and expanded in the United States, and taken to its extreme by Hitler's Nazi regime. These sources of conflict illustrate the often calamitous result of using science to justify a set of values.

Because of the controversial nature of intellectual heritability research, we review here the key points that we hope our readers will take away from this chapter. First, we presented the major questions asked by researchers interested in the heritability of intelligence, noting that these questions stem from only a subset of the metaphors—geographic and biological—that have been used to conceptualize intelligence. Research into the heritability of intelligence, therefore, is limited to these perspectives. In Chapter One, we argued that it is only through a combination of perspectives that a phenomenon as complex and wide-ranging as intelligence can truly be understood. The same is true for understanding its genetic basis. An important, but implicit, assumption here is that Spearman's g and IQ scores, on the one hand, and lifetime accomplishments, on the other, are not synonymous. The exploration of genes and intelligence, therefore, is not the same as the exploration of genes and one's capability to succeed in everyday life, which is subject to many uncontrollable environmental influences, such as country of origin, economic depression, war, and so on.

Second, we presented the methods used for understanding the degree to which differences among people can be attributed to genes versus the environment. In this section, we pointed out that, as a way of exploring heritability, pitting genes against environment is a way of exploring heritability is waning in its perceived utility (see Grigorenko, 2000). Although asking questions about the relative contributions of genes and the environment have served the scientific community well — through developments in methodology, statistical analysis, and knowledge — it has not shed light on the mechanisms through which genes have their effects on intellectual behavior.

Third, in the same section we also emphasized that discovering that differences among people in intellectual competency can be attributed to genes does not mean that people are genetically predetermined to have a particular IQ score. We noted that there is substantial interplay between genes and environment in determining one's intellectual competency, and that methods used to understand heritability apply to populations of people and not the individual members of these populations.

Fourth, we discussed the future of behavior–genetic research, the identification of the genes that contribute to intelligence and the description of the biochemical process through which genes exert their effects. In this section we emphasized that this work is yet in its infancy. Achieving a biochemical understanding of the genetic mechanisms underlying intelligence is highly complex and requires much work in exploring both biology and environments.

Finally, we cannot overemphasize the importance of the fact that science is silent with regard to social policy. None of the findings we have presented has direct implications for educators, legislators, or even parents. We hope that this chapter has helped our readers to be more critical consumers of research findings as they pertain to social policy and has inspired an interest on the part of our readers to educate themselves on these topics in more depth.

Conclusion

In this chapter we have presented the major questions asked by researchers interested in the genetic and environmental bases of intelligence. We provided an overview of the methods used to explore answers to these questions, including both behavior-genetic and molecular–genetic approaches. We briefly discussed the findings of research using these methods, emphasizing what these findings mean and do not mean scientifically. Finally, we emphasized that the controversial nature of these findings stems from the inappropriate use of science to justify choices regarding social policy.

An important controversy that we did not discuss in this chapter is that surrounding the possible genetic basis of group differences in intelligence. Although differences between different groups of people (e.g., blacks and whites, whites and Asians) on various tests of intelligence have been found, the questions about genetics raised in this chapter do not pertain to these differences. Indeed, although many explanations for group differences in intelligence have been put forth—including genetic ones—it is not yet known what accounts for them. We explore this topic in Chapter Five.

Group Differences in Intelligence

As in Chapter Four, much of the history we present in this chapter involves intelligence theory and measurement based on the geographic metaphor. That is, in explorations of group differences in intelligence, intelligence typically has been defined as Spearman's g (see Chapter One) and has been assessed using IQ tests, which are believed to be good measures of g (Jensen, 1980). Tests of abstract reasoning, such as Raven's Progressive Matrices (Raven, 1938), have also been used, as have assessments more reflective of scholastic achievement, such as the SAT (see Chapter Two). Interestingly, the origin of geographic intelligence testing in Great Britain and in the United States appears to have some basis in attempts to rank particular racial, ethnic, or socioeconomic groups according to their intelligence (Gould, 1996). Rank ordering various groups of people in terms of alleged "worth" was of particular interest before intelligence testing began (Smedley, 2002), but testing had the promise of providing a formal, scientific way to characterize how groups of people actually differed on a characteristic of great social interest.

Ranking groups of people based on the average measured intelligence of their members results, by definition, in some groups being ranked lower than others. Because intelligence is a socially valued characteristic, serving as a gateway to educational and economic opportunities and even as a criterion for self-worth, exploring group differences in intelligence has been controversial since its inception and continues to generate conflict even in modern times (e.g., contrast Herrnstein & Murray's *The Bell Curve* [1994] with Stephen J. Gould's *The Mismeasure of Man* [1996]). Controversy appears to stem not so much from findings indicating the presence of group differences but more from the explanations used to understand the findings, which are based on preconceived notions as frequently as they are based on actual scientific data.

In this chapter, we present findings regarding group differences in intelligence, as defined by the geographic metaphor. We focus our presentation on sex differences and race differences in order to feature the groups investigated in the majority of the research literature, though social-class differences and occupational differences in intelligence have also been occasionally explored. We also discuss research devoted to understanding the complex causes of these differences. With regard to race differences, our discussion focuses primarily on causes of differences in the United States, as race differences in intelligence have been of particular social concern to that country. As our readers will discover, the findings regarding group differences in geographic intelligence are rather consistent, yet relatively little is known about the nature of these differences or how to alleviate them.

Sex Differences in Intelligence

To educated men, the intellectual inferiority of women was "known" before the development of formal intelligence testing practices. Such discoveries as the closer similarity between women and "savages" than between women and "adult, civilized" men — based in part on differences in brain size, but apparently also on the word of poets and novelists — served as a justification for preventing women access to education and to participation in politics (see Gould, 1996). Modern, systematic, and much more rigorous research on intelligence differences between females and males suggests that sex differences in intelligence are relatively minor, reflected more in differences in patterns of mental abilities, rather than in overall intelligence.

Findings about sex differences

Overall Intelligence

The general consensus among psychologists is that there do not exist meaningful, systematic differences in overall intelligence among males and females, as indicated by IQ scores on such tests as the Wechsler Adult Intelligence Scale (Halpern & LaMay, 2000; Loehlin, 2000). This may be in part because IQ tests are designed to yield roughly equivalent average IQ scores for males and females by removing questions that males or females as a group have particular difficulty answering correctly. In addition, IQ tests generally feature tests of multiple intellectual abilities, including verbal ability and mathematical ability (see Chapter Two). Males and females demonstrate differing strengths in these abilities and therefore achieve similar overall scores, on average. Some researchers and test developers have found small differences in overall IQ between males and females favoring men (e.g., Loehlin, 2000; Lynn, 1994), but the average of these differences has not exceeded five IQ points. To get an appreciation for how small this difference is, an increase of five IQ points as a result of remedial education has been considered minimal improvement when considering the effectiveness of efforts to teach intelligence (see Chapter Three).

Visual–Spatial Ability

Although there are many facets of visual–spatial ability (Lohman, 1987), males typically enjoy a substantial advantage over females on most visual–spatial tasks, an advantage that first appears as early as three years of age (Halpern, 1997; Halpern & LaMay, 2000). One possible exception is tasks that require the mental imaging of complex sequences of spatial information, such as figuring out the most efficient way to untie a complicated knot or determining which supports can be removed from a structure without the structure collapsing. Verbalizing the sequences of spatial information may be helpful in solving these kinds of spatial tasks (Kyllonen, Lohman & Snow, 1984), a strategy that would be particularly useful for females, thereby reducing sex differences in performance.

Mathematical Ability

Mathematical ability, particularly mathematical reasoning, is another ability in which males enjoy a significant advantage that occurs very early in life, as early as preschool (Halpern, 1997; Halpern & LaMay, 2000). Young girls do show an advantage in mathematical computation over young boys, but this advantage becomes less salient in school settings as mathematical problem solving becomes less computation-driven and more complex and inferential (Loehlin, 2000). The male advantage in mathematical reasoning may stem, in part, from heavy reliance on spatial-visualization techniques when solving abstract mathematical reasoning problems (Halpern & LaMay, 2000). Males are also more variable in their mathematical ability, at least in the United States (Feingold, 1994; Hedges & Nowell, 1995), where the situation is such that there are more males at the high end of mathematical ability than females. An implication of this difference in variability is that universities, employers, or intellectual giftedness programs in the United States using high cutoff scores in mathematics as a criterion for acceptance wind up with a significant under-representation of women in attendance (Hedges & Nowell, 1995).

Verbal Ability

Like visual–spatial ability, verbal ability is a multidimensional capability, but on most tasks involving the use of language females typically demonstrate an advantage that appears early in life, possibly in infancy (Halpern, 1997; Halpern & LaMay, 2000). Girls acquire language sooner and develop larger vocabularies more quickly, which may account for the later female advantage in verbal fluency, reading comprehension, and writing (Halpern & LaMay, 2000). Historically, group intelligence testing for admissions or employment purposes has involved primarily multiple-choice questions (see Chapter Two), therefore excluding an important facet of intelligence in which females excel — writing. Recent additions of writing assessments to such college entrance exams as the PSAT, the SAT, and the GRE reflect attempts to improve the gender equity of these exams (Halpern & LaMay, 2000).

Memory

Memory is yet another multidimensional capability, and females typically show an advantage throughout the lifespan over males on a variety of memory tests (Halpern & LaMay, 2000). Women have demonstrated, for example, better memories for word lists, personally experienced events, novel associations (e.g., name–

face associations), and even spatial locations. There exists less evidence for a male–female difference in memory for facts, and men typically outperform women in tests of factual knowledge, especially in the math and sciences and in mechanics (e.g., Halpern, 1997; Hedges & Nowell, 1995).

Are Sex Differences Decreasing?

In mental abilities for which there are relatively substantial sex differences, such as visual–spatial ability, writing, mathematics and the sciences, sex differences have remained consistent over several decades (Halpern, 1997; Hedges & Nowell, 1995). In intellectual abilities for which there have been relatively small sex differences, such as abstract reasoning, there has been increasingly similar performance among males and females over the past several decades (see, for example, Feingold, 1988). Convergence in the abilities of males and females also appears to occur more in the average range of intelligence rather than among the intellectually gifted (Halpern, 1997). This suggests that while the average scores of males and females on particular ability tests may be getting closer, there remains greater variability among the previously higher-scoring group (e.g., males in mathematics) such that its members still achieve the highest scores (Hedges & Nowell, 1995).

Explanations for sex differences

It is a relatively easy endeavor to demonstrate that differences exist, but a much more difficult endeavor to determine *why* these differences exist. Both physiological explanations — involving genes, hormones, and brain organization — and sociological explanations — including evolutionary mechanisms, sex-typed parenting styles and gender roles, and peer pressure — for sex differences in various intellectual abilities have been put forth. As we demonstrated in Chapter Four with regard to understanding genes and intelligence, no single "nature" or "nurture" explanation is sufficient for understanding sex differences. A full understanding of sex differences requires the integration of nature and nurture, an approach we discuss below.

Physiological Explanations

Physiological explanations for sex differences in cognitive ability depend on there being systematic ways in which the physiology of males and females differs. One fundamental way in which males and females differ physiologically is in their genetic makeup. More specifically, females have two large X chromosomes, whereas males have one large X chromosome and one small Y chromosome. These chromosomal differences account for the systematic physiological differences we observe between males and females, such as reproductive systems and secondary sex characteristics (e.g., breasts, pelvis width, facial hair, etc.)

Some researchers began exploring the biological basis of sex differences in spatial ability by attempting to determine whether a recessive gene "for" high spatial ability was located on the X chromosome (see Halpern, 1986; Plomin, DeFries & McClearn, 1990). If high spatial ability were an X-linked recessive characteristic, then it would be demonstrated more frequently by males than by females. This is because a male's small Y chromosome cannot carry competing genetic information (e.g., a dominant "low-spatial-ability" gene) that could dominate a recessive "high-spatial-ability" gene if one were present on his X chromosome. Females have two X chromosomes; therefore, there is a greater likelihood that females will carry at least one dominant "low-spatial-ability" gene and thereby demonstrate low spatial ability (see Chapter Four). One example of such an X-linked recessive characteristic is color blindness, which occurs more frequently in males than females.

The possibility of a recessive high-spatial-ability gene was explored in part by comparing the frequency of high-spatial-ability females and males with the frequency that would be expected given the existence of such a gene. Other studies involved examining the spatial ability of women having only one X chromosome (i.e., women with Turner's syndrome), with the expectation that the occurrence of high spatial ability in these women would be as frequent as that in men. These investigations did not produce consistent results (Plomin, DeFries & McClearn, 1990). As discussed in Chapter Four, it is no longer accepted that a single gene can code a complex behavior such as intellectual ability so, in hindsight, the inconsistent results found are not surprising.

X chromosomes may not carry a spatial-ability gene, but the genes on the X and Y chromosomes do code for hormones — the estrogens, androgens, and progestins that all males and females possess — but in substantially different amounts. Differences in prenatal hormones may have what is called an *organizing*, or structuring, effect on brain development, which could account for mounting evidence suggesting that there are sex differences in brain organization (Allen, Richey, Chai & Gorski, 1991; Witelson, 1991) and in brain size (Ankney, 1992).

Males have been found to possess slightly larger brains relative to body size than females (Ankney, 1992), but females have been found to have a more bulbously shaped region of the brain called *splenium*, which is located in the *corpus callosum* (Allen, Richey, Chai & Gorski, 1991). The corpus callosum is a thick set of fibers connecting the left and right hemispheres of the brain, which may allow the neurological functioning of females to be distributed more evenly across the two hemispheres than that of males (Innocenti, 1994). Because females appear to show more even distribution of neurological functioning across the two hemispheres, some scientists have suggested sex differences in brain organization as an explanation for sex differences in various intellectual abilities (see Halpern, 1986; Lynn, 1994). The relative specialization of the left and right hemispheres of the brain for verbal and spatial processing, respectively, roughly reflects the dimensions of intellectual ability along which males and females excel differently.

No clear link has yet been made between hormones, structural characteristics of the brain, and the different patterns of ability strengths seen in males and females, however (Collaer & Hines, 1995). For example, it is unclear as to exactly why the more nearly even distribution of neurological functioning in females would result in higher verbal ability but lower spatial ability than in males. Current evidence cannot distinguish among the many competing explanations for the possible relation between brain organization and intellectual ability. In addition, as discussed in Chapter One, brain size has shown a moderate correlation with overall intelligence, but larger brains in males cannot explain the different patterns of intellectual ability strengths seen in males and females. Finally, scientific knowledge explicitly relating brain tissue to performance on intellectual ability tests is still largely undeveloped (see Chapter One; also Sternberg, 2000).

Hormones also have been found to have sex-typical *activating*, or more direct, effects on intellectual-task performance, even in old age (Halpern, 1997; Halpern & LaMay, 2000). For example, there is some evidence that increased levels of testosterone are associated with higher levels of performance on visual–spatial tasks and lower levels of performance on verbal tasks (Van Goozen, Cohen-Kettenis, Gooren, Frijda & Van De Poll, 1995). Just how hormone levels influence the electrochemical activity in the brain required by various intellectual tasks is unknown, however. The exact relation between hormones and intellectual abilities has not yet been established, in part because much hormone research is conducted with nonhuman animals or with people whose hormone levels are abnormal due to disease or genetic defect (Collaer & Hines, 1995; Halpern, 1997). Neither of these populations is considered to be fully representative of normally functioning humans, so the generalization of findings from research using these populations is limited.

Although the causes of sex differences in intelligence are complex and include non-biological factors, exploring the biological basis for these differences should not be completely disregarded as sexist or deterministic. This is because attempts to provide a biological explanation for sex differences in intellectual abilities provide a means for discovering the neurological structures and biochemical processes that may contribute to intellectual functioning more generally. In other words, it is perhaps through examining the differences between males and females that we will uncover the similarities among them. Consider hormones, for example. Males and females both possess all three kinds of hormone, androgens, estrogens, and progestins, only in differing amounts. By determining how different amounts of hormones affect the brain development and neurological processing of males and females differently, we may also determine how hormones work similarly in males and females to give rise to their many intellectual similarities. There is clearly much work to be done in understanding the biological factors giving rise to sex differences, and a better understanding of non-biological factors is of certain use in moving research forward.

Sociological Explanations

Biological differences between males and females surely do not tell the whole story of sex differences in intellectual ability. It is likely that anyone reading this book has already come up with a number of possible sociological explanations for such differences themselves, including the different way girls and boys are treated by parents and teachers, the different kinds of games that males and females play as children, and the different types of skills valued in men and women as adults. Psychologists, sociologists, and anthropologists have also put forth sociological explanations for sex differences in intellectual ability, as we discuss below.

Analogous to physiological explanations, sociological explanations for sex differences in intellectual ability depend on systematic differences in the socialization of males and females. Evolutionary psychologists such as David Buss (1995) suggest that one such systematic difference can be found in the division of labor in prehistoric societies, which resulted in the differential evolution of certain intellectual strengths in males and females. Buss and others argue that male involvement in hunting activities, such as navigating over long distances and bringing down animals, resulted in the development of superior spatial skills, whereas female involvement in foraging activities and childrearing did not promote such skills. This explanation is challenged by the fact that females appear to have played a role in hunting in some societies and that the non-hunting tasks that females accomplished likely did place demands on spatial ability (Halpern, 1997).

A close look at the kind of tasks that modern males and females engage in may provide some insight into why there are sex differences in intellectual strengths. From the time that children are very young, parents encourage them to engage in sex-typed activities (Lytton & Romney, 1991), which may lead to the development of different intellectual strengths in boys and girls. For example, young boys are encouraged to play with Lego building kits or erector sets and young girls to play with dolls and dollhouses. Similarly, adolescent boys are more strongly encouraged than girls to engage in more science- or mathematics-related activities. That men and women have developed substantially different interests by the time they reach college (Astin,

Sax, Korn & Mahoney, 1995) suggests that whatever differences develop early do not dissipate with time. Their research found, for example, that college-age men and women engaged considerably more frequently in sex-typical activities (e.g., video games and partying for men, pleasure reading and domestic chores for women) than sex-atypical activities.

Judith R. Harris (1995) has suggested that parental encouragement does not play a strong role in the divergent, sex-typical interests and activities of males and females. Rather, Harris asserted that social groups made up of peers are the predominant socializing influence in gender-role development. She observed that children have an adaptive propensity to form "in-groups" and "out-groups" and that sex is a fundamental distinguishing characteristic that groups form easily around at an early age. Peer groups place pressures on males and females to conform to sex-typical roles, and interests and behaviors adopted to remain a member of the group persist throughout adulthood.

Sociological explanations for sex differences in intellectual strengths present an interesting characterization of the distinct male and female worlds. Unfortunately, these explanations present us with a "chicken or egg" sort of quandary. That is, do differences in the socialization of males and females stem from biological differences, or does biology develop as an outcome of different socialization practices? It is likely that the answer to this question will never be known because it really is not the best question to ask. Like the developmental process of intelligence more generally, the development of sex differences in intelligence is a product of both biological and environmental factors. A description of the mechanisms through which biology and sociology interact to create sex differences, such as Diane F. Halpern's (1997; Halpern & LaMay, 2000) psychobiological model, will likely provide the kind of insight necessary to improve our understanding of the causes of sex differences in intellectual ability.

The Psychobiological Model of Sex Differences

Halpern's psychobiological model of sex differences shares many of the same insights as other scholars (e.g., Jensen, 1969; Scarr & McCartney, 1983) in their descriptions of how genes influence environment, which in turn affect, intellectual development.

Consider how biology and environment might work in concert to develop intellectual differences between the sexes. Prenatal and postnatal hormones play a role in the development of the brain, reproductive systems, and secondary sex characteristics. Parents, seeing the outcome of hormonal influences in their infant (i.e., male or female genitals, temperament, aggression levels, etc.), may encourage the child to engage in sex-typical activities as determined by the society in which they live and by their own interests (which may be determined, in part, by biology). Further biological development (e.g., particular brain structures) may result from the differential participation in sex-typical activities, thus enhancing skill development and further interest in the same kinds of activities. Sex-linked interests may then play a role in how the adult males and females raise their own children. Halpern (1997) argues that the continuing interplay of biology and sociology makes it impossible to distinguish the independent influence of either on sex differences.

Focusing on the differences between males and females may obscure the fact that there are as many similarities as differences in the intellectual capability of males and females, and could lead to the false conclusion that there is a "smarter" sex (Halpern, 1986, 1997). Our above discussion of sex differences in intelligence should demonstrate that males and females, on average, possess complementary constellations of intellectual abilities and that to try to determine which sex has "more" or "better" intelligence would be meaningless. It may happen that a particular society comes to value one type of ability over another, but this does not mean a particular sex is inferior. This preference instead suggests that the society has failed to balance its values in accordance with the particular strengths and potential contributions of both sexes (Halpern, 1997).

In addition, focusing on males and females as "groups" could draw attention away from the individuals who make up these groups—individuals who are more different from each other than the groups themselves are different (Jensen, 1980). That females have, on average, better writing skills than males, for example, does not mean that a man cannot excel at writing or that a woman cannot write a lousy essay. We can think of numerous examples of both situations! The danger of exploring group differences is that self-fulfilling prophecies or gender-related attitudes based on findings about group differences could potentially limit the achievement of boys or girls in many areas (e.g., Steele, 1997). The risk of focusing on sex differences in intelligence, however, should not outweigh the benefit to scientific knowledge that can be reaped through conducting research to understand the nature of these differences. Such knowledge is largely unavailable at this time, but could eventually promote a better understanding of how the sexes develop intellectually and what role society plays in that development.

Race Differences in Intelligence

Before beginning our discussion of race differences in intelligence, we must note that there is disagreement as to whether race is a biologically meaningful concept. Many scientists agree that race cannot be defined as a biological category with distinct boundaries, but that there is some biological basis for making fuzzy distinctions between racial groups (Loehlin, Gardner & Spuhler, 1975; Arthur R. Jensen, in Miele, 2002). However, many have also argued that race is biologically meaningless (e.g., Fish, 2002), including the American Anthropological Association (Petit, 1998).

Without a clear consensus on the existence of racial categories, let alone how to define what they are, understanding the findings from research exploring race differences can be difficult. In psychological studies, race is often indicated by research participants themselves who, depending on their country of origin, may have differing conceptualizations of racial categories (Fish, 2002) or who may have adopted conceptualizations of categories that are based on sociopolitical procedures (e.g., that a person with one white parent and one black parent is somehow "black") rather than on biological criteria. The designation of "race" in these studies therefore corresponds to a complex amalgamation of biology, culture, and possibly socioeconomic status (Helms, 1997).

The studies that we present in this chapter rely on participants' self-reports of their racial identity, and are based on the belief that some kind of biological distinction can be made between races. Given the above-stated concerns about racial categories, our use of the term "race" throughout the rest of this chapter is meant to reflect a somewhat loose composition of racial–ethnic ancestry and sociological construction. Interpretations of the findings we present and the explanations for the findings we discuss should therefore be made with this broad conceptualization of race in mind. The terms we use for race categories (e.g., white or black) are intended to reflect our respect for the wide variety of nationalities represented by people assigned to particular racial categories (e.g., many "African Americans" are not of African descent), and is consistent with the guidelines of the American Psychological Association (2001).

That there could be race differences in intelligence-test scores feels threatening in a world where races were rank ordered in terms of "worth" and intelligence before intelligence was ever formally measured (Galton, 1869; Smedley, 2002), and where being of a race of low supposed worth or intelligence meant a lifetime of subjugation, abuse, or slavery. Indeed, early assessment of intellectual differences between races via measures of brain size appears to have been conducted to provide alleged "scientific evidence" for the rank order of races that was already believed to exist. This was not an auspicious start to the modern practice of studying race differences in intelligence! Moreover, intelligence tests revealing racial and ethnic differences do have a history of being used as justifications for restricting access to school and work, preventing entry into the United States, even limiting reproductive freedom. This history, which grates against the democratic principles many people now hold dear, should serve as an admonition that, like many other scientific–technological advancements (e.g., nuclear energy), intelligence tests can be used for good or for ill.

We do not believe that race differences in intelligence test scores indicate that intelligence testing is, by definition, a racist practice. Racism occurs not in finding differences but in interpreting differences on the basis of racial prejudices rather than on the basis of scientific data. We believe that developing a thorough, honest understanding of the race differences that occur on intelligence tests will provide information about cultural, educational, and other inequities present in a society. Such an exploration may also inform our understanding of the biological basis of intelligence and provide insight into how we have come to define what intelligence, and race, really is.

Findings about race differences

Although finer distinctions are made for other kinds of psychological study, five broad categories of race are generally used in the study of group differences in intelligence: white, black, Hispanic, Native American, and Asian. It must be noted that these categories are extremely broad and vague. For example, Cubans, Puerto Ricans, Dominicans, Mexicans, Guatemalans, and Spaniards, are all "Hispanic," but of very different ethnic and cultural origins. We present general findings about group differences and then we discuss the possible complex causes for these differences. Our discussion focuses in particular on American white–black differences as a reflection of the focus present in the research literature. In our presentation of group differences, it is important to consider that these differences correspond to differences in *averages*, and do not refer to all members of any particular group. Therefore, it is not the case that *all* members of a lower-scoring group score lower than *all* of the members of a higher-scoring group. Rather, there are many people in lower-scoring groups who achieve the same scores or even outperform members of higher-scoring groups (see figure 5.1).This is as true for the sex differences presented above as it is for the race differences presented below.

White–Black Differences

Historically, in the United States, whites have scored, on average, approximately 15 IQ points higher than blacks on intelligence tests (e.g., Jensen, 1980; Loehlin, Gardner & Spuhler, 1975; Roth, Bevier, Bobko, Switzer & Tyler, 2001). However, there is recent evidence that this difference has been decreasing since 1965 (Hedges & Nowell, 1998). Whites also are more variable in IQ scores than blacks, resulting in relatively more whites at the highest-scoring end of tests of intellectual ability (analogous to males on tests of mathematical ability, see above, also Hedges & Nowell, 1995, 1998). This difference in variability between the two racial groups does not appear to be decreasing (Hedges & Nowell, 1998). Finally, there is some indication that the difference between whites and blacks is greater on tests that are more complex and better measures of Spearman's g, such as abstract

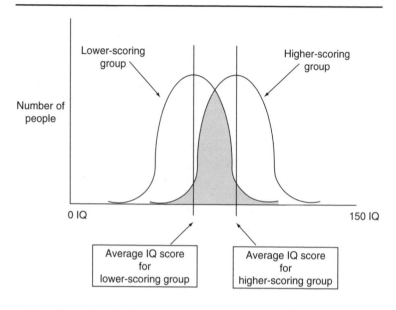

Note: Shaded area indicates overlap between higher- and lower-scoring groups
(i.e., people from different groups achieving the same score)

Figure 5.1   *Overlap of Lower-Scoring and Higher-Scoring Groups on an IQ Test*

reasoning, than on less complex tests of intellectual ability, such as tests of memory or perceptual speed (Jensen, 1985; Vernon & Jensen, 1984). Some evidence suggests, however, that the greater difference observed on tests of abstract reasoning than on tests of memory or perceptual speed may be due not to differences in race but to differences in socioeconomic status that are often associated with race (Humphreys, 1985).

White–Hispanic Differences

Our Hispanic designation corresponds to a group of people whose members come from very diverse cultural backgrounds (i.e., Mexicans, Central and South Americans, Puerto Ricans, and Cubans), but who are unified in their rapidly increasing emigration to the United States and the consequent challenges they experience trying to adapt to a new culture and language. The intelligence-test scores of whites and Hispanics differ by approximately 11 IQ points (Roth, Bevier, Bobko, Switzer & Tyler, 2001; Sackett, Schmitt, Ellingson & Kabin, 2001), on average, with greater differences on tests with predominantly verbal content than on other tests of intellectual ability (Neisser, Boodoo, Bouchard, et al., 1996). That white–Hispanic differences are greater on tests of verbal ability is not surprising, given the linguistic challenges experienced by Hispanics but not by most whites.

White–Native American Differences

Like Hispanics, Native Americans are widely diverse in their culture and language. In addition, Native Americans vary widely in their geographic location, with resulting differences in ecology (e.g., compare the living conditions of the Inuit [Eskimos] in Alaska to the Navajos in Arizona) and therefore differences in opportunities to develop particular intellectual abilities. Although relatively few definitive studies of differences in the intellectual abilities of whites and Native Americans have been conducted, some consistent results have emerged.

Native Americans — like Hispanics — tend to perform as well as whites on tests of visual–spatial ability, but substantially less well than whites on tests of verbal ability (Lynn, 1991). In the case of Native Americans, as with the Hispanics, differences in verbal ability may be, in part, due to having greater difficulty with the English language. Native American children also experience a greater incidence of chronic middle-ear infection than other children, and the resulting hearing loss has been associated with lower verbal IQ scores (McShane & Plas, 1984). Interestingly, the Inuit appear to have particularly high visual–spatial abilities with minimal sex differences, possibly a result of the ecological demands present in the environments where they live (McShane & Berry, 1988; see also anthropological theories of intelligence in Chapter One).

White–Asian Differences

To those who have read about or personally witnessed the academic and technical excellence generally associated with Asians, it may come as a surprise that there is disagreement among psychologists regarding the size and nature of differences between Asians and whites in intelligence-test scores. Some investigations have revealed an average IQ for Asians that is several points higher than the average IQ of whites (Lynn, 1991, 1993), but other investigations have revealed an average IQ that is a few points lower (Flynn, 1991). Another investigation revealed hardly any white–Asian difference in intellectual abilities at all (Stevenson, Stigler, Lee, Lucker, Kitamura & Hsu, 1985). Evidence also exists suggesting that, like Hispanics and native Americans, Asians show slightly worse performance, on average, on tests of verbal ability than whites (Nagoshi & Johnson, 1987). Of course, these tests are in English, not in Asian languages!

Whether the IQ scores of Asians are slightly higher, slightly lower, or the same as those of whites, whatever difference does exist fails to account for substantial Asian superiority in academic achievement (e.g., grades and achievement tests, such as the SAT) and the predominance of Asians in many science- and mathematics-related professions (Flynn, 1991). This failure highlights the distinction between intelligence tests and achievement tests in Chapter Two, and indicates that such factors as hard work, attitude toward learning, and possibly temperament may play a role above and beyond geographic intelligence in lifetime achievement (Neisser, Boodoo, Bouchard, et al., 1996).

Explanations for race differences

Just as certainty about race differences in intelligence preceded the measurement of intelligence, certainty about the causes of race differences in intelligence has often preceded the relevant scientific research into the matter (Lewontin, 1970). These explanations range from genetics, to socioeconomic and cultural factors, to characteristics of the test-taking situation. We discuss each of these explanations in turn, with, perhaps not surprisingly, an emphasis on the complexity of causes in race differences in intelligence-test scores.

Genetics

One of the most controversial events in the history of psychology was the 1969 publication of a lengthy article in the *Harvard Educational Review* in which Arthur R. Jensen promoted a possible genetic explanation for race differences (in particular white–

black differences) in tested intelligence. In his article, Jensen connected, among other facts, the resistance of the black–white difference in IQ scores to compensatory education (e.g., Head Start) with the substantial heritability of intelligence (see Chapter Four), and concluded that genetics were "strongly implicated" (p. 82) in race differences in intelligence. Jensen also discussed the social implications of the possible genetic basis of race differences, suggesting, for example, that black and white children should receive different educations suited to their abilities. This article received a very strong negative reaction among other scientists and among the public, resulting in the publication of several articles and books debating the veracity of "Jensenism," or the belief that IQ differences between races are inherited genetically. Decades later, the controversy remains, kept alive by such books as *The Bell Curve* (Herrnstein & Murray, 1994), whose authors support Jensen's ideas, and *The Mismeasure of Man* (Gould, 1996), whose author did not. The controversy also remains in the scholarly literature (Rushton & Jensen, in press; Sternberg, in press).

Currently, there exists no evidence that can definitively answer the question of whether or not race differences in intelligence have a genetic basis (e.g., see Neisser, Boodoo, Bouchard et al., 1996). In order for there to be a genetic basis for race differences in intelligence, two fundamental questions must be answered in the affirmative. The first of these questions is: "Are there genetically distinguishable races?" The answer to this question is: "Yes and no."

Groups of people are considered genetically different if they possess differing *gene frequencies*, which are occurrences of genes such as those that code for skin color, facial structure, and so on (Loehlin, Gardner, Spuhler, 1975). For example, a member of a group of people existing in a very hot climate (e.g., Saharan Africa) will more likely possess the genes that code for long limbs and lanky bodies than a member of a group existing in some other climate. In contrast, a member of a group of people existing in a very cold climate (e.g., the Arctic Circle) will more likely possess the genes that code for short limbs and rounded bodies. However, many, if not most, characteristics that we observe to be different among groups of people are coded by multiple genes (i.e., they are polygenic, see Chapter Four), which likely overlap tremendously among all people. Moreover, gradual changes in gene frequency across groups of people living in neighboring geographic regions make "pure" races an impossibility (Loehlin, Gardner & Spuhler, 1975).

There are some differences in the frequency of single-gene characteristics, however, that are associated with people who already belong to existing racial categories. For example, blacks are significantly more likely to be carriers of the gene for sickle-cell anemia than are people of other races, indicating that this gene has a greater frequency in the black population than in other populations. This information is used by the medical community to provide genetic screening for black parents (Plomin, DeFries & McClearn, 1990), and suggests that meaningful information about genetic differences between races can be discovered and put to good use.

The sorting of people into one racial category or another, even when the criterion for sorting is the frequency of a particular gene, is largely arbitrary (Loehlin, Gardner & Spuhler, 1975). That is, depending on the genes selected, different "races" can be formed, such as the races of "Lankys" and "Roundeds" (see Fish, 2002) based on the gene frequencies described in our example above. That said, racial distinctions have long been made among people of differing physical characteristics and these distinctions have often had meaningful social implications, independent of their biological veracity. In order to understand current racial differences in intelligence, the problem is not so much to determine whether genetically distinct races can be identified but rather to determine whether the races that have already been identified are genetically distinct in ways that are meaningful with regard to intelligence.

Therefore, the second fundamental question underlying race differences in intelligence is: "Do differences in gene frequencies between the already existing 'races' involve genes that are involved in intelligent behavior?" The answer to this question is: "Nobody knows." As described in Chapter Four, the genes involved in intelligent behavior are currently unknown. Research that will answer this question is still in its infancy, so it cannot yet be known whether different races have differing frequencies of "intelligence" genes. No evidence has been found that they do or that they do not.

It may be difficult to understand how intelligence could be highly heritable within a particular group of people (see Chapter Four), but that race differences in intelligence could potentially have no basis in genetics. To understand this, consider taking two handfuls of genetically variable corn seed, planting each handful in a field of different soil quality, and then, after several weeks, measuring the height of the corn plants (see also Lewontin, 1970). *Within* each field, variation in corn height will be highly heritable because the environment in which the corn grew (i.e., soil quality) was the same for all of the seeds but the genetic makeup of the seeds was different. *Across* the two fields, variation in corn height will be largely attributable to differences in the soil quality between the two fields in which the corn was planted. This is because the genetic makeup of the two handfuls of seed was highly similar.

The extrapolation of this example to race differences in intelligence—particularly white–black differences in the United States—is obvious. It is likely that the "fields" in which many black children grow up have differing "soil quality" than those in which many white children grow up. That there are environmental factors contributing to the persistent race differences in intelligence-test scores is widely accepted (Neisser, Boodoo, Bouchard, 1996). However, relatively few people have explicitly identified features of the environment that differ between races, and described how these differences affect the development of intelligence (Mandler, 2001). The result is that it has been difficult to demonstrate scientifically the influence that environments surely have on race differences in intelligence test scores, or to improve intelligence by enhancing these environments (Jensen, 1969; Ogbu, 1986). For example, relatively broad characterizations of racial differences in socioeconomic status (SES)—and consequent differences in living conditions, such as access to schooling, and nutrition—have not been able to explain race differences in intelligence because such differences persist even when blacks and whites are equated on SES (Loehlin, Gardner & Spuhler, 1975).

Caste Systems

Some insight into the role of environmental factors in North American race differences in intelligence has come from the study of racial or ethnic groups in other countries, specifically groups that comprise caste systems (Ogbu, 1986; Ogbu & Stern, 2001). Over several decades of cross-cultural research,

John U. Ogbu noted the similarity of American race differences in intelligence to the differences in intelligence found between members of higher- and lower-levels of caste systems in such countries as India, Israel, Japan, and New Zealand. Race was not necessarily the criterion used for sorting people into the castes that Ogbu studied, yet the differences in test scores and school achievement were quite similar. In addition, Ogbu noted that many political, social, and economic difficulties experienced by members of the castes he studied were similar to those experienced by blacks in the United States.

Ogbu (1986) distinguished between three types of minority in the United States: immigrant minorities, autonomous minorities, and caste-like minorities. Immigrant minorities are people who have emigrated voluntarily to the United States in order to improve their economic, political, or social situation. These minorities see participation in education and in the American economic system as instrumental in achieving their goals, though they always retain the option of returning to the countries they left. Although often holding menial jobs and living in poorer living conditions than the majority group, immigrant minorities see themselves as better off than their peers still living in their homelands. Autonomous minorities, such as the Amish or the Mormons, also live voluntarily in the United States, but do not experience the same economic or social subordination of immigrant minorities. These minorities may experience discrimination but, like the immigrant minorities, they see participation in the educational and economic systems in the United States as instrumental to success. Caste-like minorities are unique in that their participation in American educational and economic systems is involuntary. These minorities have either been taken to the United States involuntarily through, for example, slavery, or have otherwise been permanently relegated to the bottom rungs of the social, political, and economic ladders. Because caste-like minorities acquire their status at birth and feel powerless to improve their position in society, they do not share the same attitudes toward education and economic participation that other minorities do. In contrast, they see developing collective identities and manipulating the system as more instrumental in achieving success.

Ogbu (1986) identified several caste-like minorities in the United States, including blacks, Native Americans, Mexicans, native Hawaiians, and Puerto Ricans, who share features with the "untouchables" in India, non-European Jews in Israel, and the Burakumin in Japan. He also identified several negative implications of being a caste-like minority for succeeding in intelligence testing situations. For example, Obgu and Stern (2001) recently observed that the IQ scores of black Americans do not necessarily reflect the "best they can do" intellectually because caste-like minority status is the foundation for the socialization practices in black communities with regard to testing and intelligence. Ogbu and Stern observed that black Americans are often skeptical of whether benefit is truly linked to performing well on IQ tests. This skepticism comes from both individual and collective experiences in which cognitive ability testing was used as a discriminatory device and test scores showed no relation to educational or occupational outcomes. Also, forced immigration and over 200 years of discriminatory practices have fostered an unwillingness to adopt "white ways," which include language and other academic skills required in testing situations (see also Herbert, 2003). The attitudes arising from these socialization practices have implications for the kinds of instructional practices taking place in the homes of black Americans and their consequences of these practices in terms of test scores.

Test Bias

Rather than targeting different developmental factors as explanations for race differences in intelligence-test scores, many have raised concerns about the testing situation itself. That mental testing is biased against racial, cultural, or ethnic minorities has been put forth as an explanation for group differences since the creation of formal intelligence and scholastic achievement tests (Jensen, 1980), and still exists in modern times (e.g., Helms, 1997). A tricky characteristic of test bias is that it is defined differently by test takers and test-development experts.

Common, everyday use of the term "test bias" generally refers to testing situations in which there is a disproportionate number of people in a particular group giving the wrong answers to the questions, and this difference is due not to ability differences but to differences in acculturation. According to this definition, an example of a biased test question might be the following verbal analogy: "Harry Potter is to Voldemort as Ronald Reagan is to

(A) California; (B) President; (C) John Hinckley; or (D) Reaga-nomics." A person unfamiliar with either J. K. Rowling's Harry Potter stories or United States' history would be unable to answer this analogy correctly without guessing because he would not know that Voldemort attempted to kill Harry Potter, as John Hinckley attempted to assassinate Ronald Reagan. An entire test made up of such questions would produce systematically lower scores for people who were not familiar with the necessary information, even though the ability of these people to complete verbal analogies may comparable to those who were. Similarly, if an intelligence or achievement test contains several questions that systematically make answering difficult for a particular racial, ethnic, or socioeconomic group, such that the intelligence of that group appears falsely lower, the test is believed to be biased.

Currently, there are no objective criteria for determining—before a test is administered—whether its questions are cultur-ally biased. Put in other words, the only way to determine if a question is biased is to use the exact same evidence that could also be used to determine that there are actual group differences in intelligence—differing proportions of people in each group getting the test questions correct. Systematic, objective criteria for determining test bias during the test-development process would allow test developers to eliminate biased test questions proactively and to the benefit of all racial, ethnic, or socioeco-nomic groups. Attempts to create "culture-reduced" intelligence tests have been made (e.g., Cattell & Cattell, 1963) but, interest-ingly, race differences tend to be larger on tests of this nature than on more "culturally loaded" tests (Jensen, 1980; though see Humphreys, 1985).

Test-development experts take a different view of test bias, using more objective, statistical terms. Because the primary pur-pose of intelligence tests is to predict such socially relevant outcomes as educational achievement, they define a test as biased if it systematically makes different predictions for differ-ent groups of people. This would occur, for example, if the academic achievement of blacks were actually higher than what the scores of blacks on IQ tests would actually predict. In such a case, blacks would not be admitted to particular schools or pro-grams on the basis of test scores that are not reflective of what black students would actually do in the schools or programs.

Psychologists studying intelligence generally agree that intelligence tests are not biased in this statistical, predictive sense (Jensen, 1980; Neisser, Boodoo, Bouchard, 1996; though see Melnick, 1997).

It should be self-evident that using intelligence-test scores as proxies for "worth" is a misguided practice, but scores on relatively narrow measures of intelligence such as tests of Spearman's g do show a relation to numerous criteria of social value (Ree & Caretta, 2002). That groups of people who have, on average, lower IQ scores experience, on average, reduced health and fitness, lower occupational status, and increased crime rates highlights the critical social importance of understanding the complex web of possible biological and societal causes for race differences in intelligence. It is a web we currently know little about.

At this time, the nature of the relation between intelligence and socially valued criteria cannot be determined from the available data. It is unknown, for example, whether having lower intelligence causes people to commit crimes, whether growing up surrounded by crime hinders intellectual development, or whether some third factor accounts for link between low intelligence and crime. Failure to study race differences for fear of finding them, however, will force these important issues to remain in the dark at the cost of the people who stand to benefit the most. Worse is the failure to rigorously study the causes of race differences because it is believed they are already known. The consequence of such ignorance is pseudoscientific theories about the genetic inferiority of particular races, failed intervention programs based on fad theories of environmental factors in intellectual development, and continued inability to alleviate social inequities. Further research into the nature of intelligence, its genetic, biological, and social basis, its enhancement, and its measurement will not only enhance our scientific knowledge, but improve the world we live in as well.

Conclusion

In this chapter, we have discussed sex differences and race differences in intelligence and the possible causes for these differences that have been put forth. We have emphasized that these causes are complex and that there is much research yet to be done in order to fully understand them. Although other group differences in intelligence have been explored (e.g., occupational differences and social class differences), we focused on sex and race differences because of their particular relevance to social concerns in the United States and because of the continuing challenges in understanding the causes of these differences.

It should be emphasized at the closing of a chapter on group differences in intelligence that there is substantially more variability within groups than between them (Jensen, 1980), such that it is impossible to make conclusions about individual people on the basis of their group membership. It should also be emphasized that the differences between groups on intelligence tests are often small, and do not represent prophecies for group differences in lifetime achievement. Finally, we wish to emphasize that group differences have been assessed in intelligence as defined and measured using the geographic metaphor. Geographic theories and tests of intelligence do not capture all that humans do intellectually, and assessments based on other intelligence theories or testing practices may show reduced group differences.

Concluding Remarks

In this short book we have tried to present a brief history of thinking about intelligence, and have hopefully demonstrated that this history was shaped by the different ways that scholars have conceptualized the nature of intelligence. Unfortunately, because our presentation was brief, we were obligated to discuss only a fraction of the intelligence research that has been conducted. We selected the studies and programs that we felt best represented the work in a particular area and we tried to present a balanced view of some of the more controversial topics in intelligence research. It should be evident by the conclusion of this book that the field of intelligence research is quite diverse, not only in approaches used to explore the nature of intelligence but also in the ways that knowledge about intelligence is applied to measurement and instruction. We hope that our readers can come away from this book with a deeper understanding of these topics and a desire to explore them in more depth.

We also hope that we have demonstrated how far scholarly knowledge about intelligence extends beyond what is generally known to the public. Mainstream literature discussing intelligence is still dominated by a limited number of the metaphors used to conceptualize intelligence: the geographic, computational, and biological metaphors (e.g., see Deary, 2001). Most intelligence tests administered to schoolchildren and adults are based on the geographic metaphor, and much of the controversy about intelligence has surrounded research stemming from the geographic and biological metaphors. We have tried to demonstrate that the history of intelligence is replete with diverse perspectives on what intelligence is, how it should be measured, and whether it can be taught. The field of intelligence is relatively young — it has only existed since the latter half of the nineteenth century — and therefore there is much learning to be done before intelligence can be fully understood.

Finally, we hope that our readers have gained an understanding that there are many more questions about intelligence than there are answers. Intelligence has been a topic of interest among philosophers, employers, educators, psychologists, anthropologists, computer scientists, and laypeople that extends back thousands of years. With so much research yet to conduct, this interest likely will extend long into the future. It seems fitting to end this book, therefore, with our ideas for where the future can (or should) take intelligence research. Below, we briefly describe the intelligence theories, measurement, and instructional interventions that we see developing in the future. We also share our insights regarding further development in research exploring the genetic basis of intelligence and the causes for group differences in intelligence.

Future Theories

The theories of intelligence that we discussed in Chapter One of this book are widely diverse. Yet, intelligence theorists seem to agree on what the overarching purpose of intelligence is: adaptation to the environment (Neisser, Boodo, Bouchard, et al., 1996). The biggest hurdle that future theories of intelligence must leap, then, is determining what exactly "the environment" is, and how adaptation occurs (Kirlik, in press; Mandler, 2001). More recent theories of intelligence, such as those based on the sociological, anthropological, and systems metaphors, have had the characterization of environments and adaptive mechanisms as an explicit component. But this work must be extended by a theory of environments in order to develop a systematic understanding of how differences between environments in fostering or demanding intelligence correspond to differences between people in demonstrating intelligent behavior (see Kirlik, in press).

Future intelligence theories must also leap the hurdle of intellectual development. Specifically, they must reveal the correspondence between the development of intelligent capability and the development of the specific neurological structures (e.g., Garlick, 2002). In addition, these theories must illuminate the role that interests, motivation, and learning dispositions play in intellectual development. Pioneering work in this area has already been done (e.g., Ackerman, 1996), but it must be extended before we can fully understand the chain of events that leads to a particular person's demonstrated intelligence.

Future Measurement

The future of intelligence testing should be an interesting one indeed. We believe that as research based on the sociological and systems metaphors continues, there will be a corresponding increase in the prevalence and sophistication of tests based on these metaphors. Much of the future of intelligence measurement will be made by advances in dynamic testing (see Sternberg & Grigorenko, 2002) and the construction and refinement of test batteries based on the systems metaphor (e.g., Sternberg & the Rainbow Project Collaborators, in press). We expect that as systems theories of intelligence more precisely articulate the range of intellectual activities that people can engage in, innovations in testing will provide a means for systematically measuring a wider array of intellectual capability. Advancements in computer simulation (Rothrock & Kirlik, 2003) and other media (Olson-Buchanan, Drasgow, Moberg, Mead, Patricia & Donovan, 1998) already make it possible to assess knowledge and skills in ways not previously believed possible.

Of course, we also believe that there will be developments in testing that are based on the geographic metaphor. Even now we are seeing how recent advances in statistical analysis are helping to design geographic-theory-based intelligence tests that are quicker to administer and better suited to the abilities of examinees (Drasgow, Levine & Zickar, 1996). Further development of traditional intelligence tests will allow finer and finer discriminations to be made among people, discriminations that will be useful for diagnosing intellectual deficiencies and prescribing remedial treatment.

Future Instructional Interventions

Much of the research evaluating the efficacy of attempts to teach intelligence has concluded with the observation that long-term, intensive instructional programs are the most successful. Yet, the number of studies implementing and rigorously evaluating such programs is few. In addition, even the most successful programs to teach intelligence often fail to have long-term or wide-ranging benefits, when such benefits are evaluated.

Future research into the teachability of intelligence should therefore have a greater focus on integrating instructional interventions seamlessly into the schools and on developing rigorous methods for evaluating the efficacy of the interventions on several occasions. Smaller-scale studies conducted outside of the immediate school environment should seek to illuminate the dispositional and environmental factors that play a role in human intellectual development and should therefore be fostered in the classroom (Grotzer & Perkins, 2000).

Future Genetic Research

Scientific knowledge about genes and their role in human development grows daily. We have no doubt that future exploration of the genetic basis of intelligence will be one of the most rapidly changing fronts in intelligence research. Now that estimates of heritability have demonstrated convincingly that genes play a substantial role in intelligent behavior, research efforts will focus more on developing cost-effective methods for identifying the many genes involved in intelligence and determining their relative levels of influence (Grigorenko, 2000). In addition, research in a field called *functional genomics* will focus on unraveling the complex process through which genes influence behavior (Plomin, 2002). Functional genomics involves tracing the path of gene products, such as protein, through cells and cell systems. The cell systems of particular interest to intelligence research are, of course, those that make up the brain.

Because prior research has also demonstrated convincingly that genes and environments jointly influence intelligent behavior, continued research into the genetic basis of intelligence must also involve the exploration of environments (e.g., see Mandler, 2001). Although the influence of some environmental factors has been examined (e.g., number of books in the home, socioeconomic status, education level of the parents), it is largely unknown what specific environmental conditions help or hinder the development of intelligence. Findings regarding the teachability of intelligence, discussed in Chapter Three, and regarding group differences in intelligence, discussed in the previous chapter, suggest some places to begin more in-depth exploration — such as the factors in home environments or cultural communities that foster dispositions for or against learning.

Future Understanding of Group Differences

Group differences in intelligence test scores have been shown consistently for nearly as long as intelligence tests have been administered. Over time, however, the size and nature of these differences have changed. For example, in the early 1900s Jews who emigrated to the United States performed, on average, poorly on IQ tests relative to non-Jewish American-born children. More recent investigation has shown that Jews now outscore non-Jewish Americans on standardized intelligence tests (Reeve & Milton, 2002). As discussed in Chapter Five, sex differences in some abilities have shrunk since the 1960s. On the basis of this evidence, it will be worthwhile for future research into group differences to take several directions, with the goal of understanding the complex causes of these differences and methods for further reducing them.

First, researchers should work together to set more rigorous definitions of race such that racial categories selected by research participants will have consistent, reliable meaning across studies. Since racial definitions cannot be based on biology alone (Fish, 2002), precise societal definitions of race should be determined and their link to biological factors made clear. A more precise definition of race would pave the way for the second future research direction, better characterization of the specific environmental factors that play a role in intellectual development (described above) and clearer links between intelligence and the biological factors involved in societal definitions of race. Future research into the causes for sex differences will also benefit from a clearer understanding of the joint effects of biology and environment, as outlined in Halpern & LaMay (2000). A third important research direction involves the creation of intelligence tests that show reduced group differences (e.g., see Sternberg & the Rainbow Project Collaborators, in press) and an evaluation of the relevance of the intellectual capabilities they measure to success at work and in everyday life (Sackett, Schmitt, Ellingson & Lamon, 2001).

Although scholarly thinking about intelligence has an illustrious history, there has never been a more exciting time than the present to explore the many facets of intelligent behavior. We have listed above only some general directions we believe future intelligence research will take, with full knowledge that there will always be more to study than there are time and resources to study it. Through the integration of multiple ideas and approaches and the collaboration of scholars in different disciplines, however, our knowledge will continue to grow and scientific understanding will maintain its crucial forward direction.

References

Ackerman, P. L. 1988. Determinants of individual differences during skill acquisition: Cognitive abilities and information processing. *Journal of Experimental Psychology: General* 117(3): 288–318.

—— 1996. A theory of adult intellectual development: Process, personality, interests, and knowledge. *Intelligence* 22: 227–57.

Ackerman, P. L. & Cianciolo, A. T. 1999. Psychomotor abilities via touchpanel testing: Measurement innovations, construct, and criterion validity. *Human Performance* 123(3/4): 231–73.

Allen, L. S., Richey, M. F., Chai, Y. M. & Gorski, R. A. 1991. Sex differences in the corpus callosum of the living human being. *The Journal of Neuroscience* 11: 933–42.

American Psychological Association. 2001. *Publication manual of the American Psychological Association* 5th ed. Washington, DC: American Psychological Association.

Anderson, J. R. 1983. *The architecture of cognition.* Cambridge, MA: Harvard University Press.

Anderson, J. R. & Schunn, C. D. 2000. Implications of the ACT-R theory: No magic bullets. In R. Glaser, ed., *Advances in instructional psychology: Educational design and cognitive science*, pp. 1–33. Mahwah, NJ: Lawrence Erlbaum Associates.

Andrade, H. G. & Perkins, D. N. 1998. Learnable intelligence and intelligent learning. In R. J. Sternberg & W. M. Williams, eds., *Intelligence, instruction, and assessment*, pp. 67–94. Mahwah, NJ: Lawrence Erlbaum Associates.

Ankney, C. D. 1992. Sex differences in relative brain size: The mismeasure of women too? *Intelligence* 16: 329–36.

Astin, A., Sax, L., Korn, W. & Mahoney, K. 1995. *The American freshman: National norms for fall 1995.* Los Angeles: Higher Education Research Institute.

Azuma, H. & Kashiwagi, K. 1987. Descriptions for an intelligent person: A Japanese study. *Japanese Psychological Research* 29: 17–26.

Baddeley, A. D. 1986. "Working memory and learning." In *Working memory*. Oxford Psychology Series vol. 11, pp. 33–53. Oxford: Oxford University Press (Clarendon).

Baltes, P. B. & Willis, S. L. 1982. Plasticity and enhancement of intellectual functioning in old age: Penn State's Adult Development and Enrichment Project (Project ADEPT). In E. I. M. Craik & S. Trehub, eds., *Aging and cognitive processes*, pp. 353–89. New York: Plenum Press.

Baron, J. B. & Sternberg, R. J., eds. 1987, *Teaching thinking skills: Theory and Practice*. New York: W. H. Freeman.

Berry, J. W. 1974. Radical cultural relativism and the concept of intelligence. In J. W. Berry & P. R. Dasen, eds., *Culture and cognition: Readings in cross-cultural psychology*, pp. 225–9. London: Methuen.

—— 2004. An ecocultural perspective on the development of competence. In R. J. Sternberg & E. L. Grigorenko, eds., *Culture and competence*. Washington, DC: American Psychological Association.

Bezruczko, N., Kurland, M. & Eckert, K. 1996. Elementary classroom practices show empirical relations to long-term benefits of early intervention: Sustaining the effects of early intervention. A Symposium at the Head Start 3rd National Research Conference, Washington, DC, June 20–3.

Binet, A. [1909] 1975. *Modern ideas about children*. Paris: Translated by S. Heisler. Ernest Flammarion.

Binet, A. & Simon, T. 1905. Méthodes nouvelles pour le diagnostic du niveau intellectuel des anormaux. *L'Année Psychologique*, 11: 191–244.

—— 1916. *The intelligence of the feeble-minded*. Translated by E. S. Kite. Baltimore, MD: Williams & Wilkins.

Blagg, N. 1991. *Can we teach intelligence? A comprehensive evaluation of Feuerstein's Instrumental Enrichment program*. Hillsdale, NJ: Lawrence Erlbaum Associates.

Blieszner, R., Willis, S. L. & Baltes, P. B. 1981. Training research on induction ability in aging: A short-term longitudinal study. *Journal of Applied Developmental Psychology*, 2: 247–65.

Blinkhorn, S. F. 1995. Burt and the early history of factor analysis. In N. Mackintosh, ed., *Cyril Burt: Fraud or framed?* London: Oxford University Press.

Block, N. 1995. How heritability misleads about race. *Cognition*, 56: 99–128.

Boas, F. 1911. *The mind of primitive man*. New York: Macmillan.

Boring, E. G. 1950. *A history of experimental psychology*. New York: Appleton-Century-Crofts.

Bouchard, T. J. & McGue, M., 1981. Familial studies of intelligence: A review. *Science*, 212: 1055–9.

Brown, A. L. & Campione, J. C. 1994. Guided discovery in a community of learners. In K. McGilly, ed., *Classroom lessons: Integrating cognitive theory and classroom practice*. Cambridge, MA: MIT Press.

Bumiller, E. 2003. "Bush seeks big changes in Head Start, drawing criticism from program's supporters." *The New York Times* July 8.

Bunge, S. A., Ochsner, K. N., Desmond, J. E., Glover, G. H. & Gabrieli, J. D. E. 2001. Prefrontal regions involved in keeping information in and out of mind. *Brain*, 124: 2074–86.

Burks, B. 1928. The relative influence of nature and nurture upon mental development: A comparative study of foster parent–foster child resemblance and true parent–true child resemblance. *27th Yearbook of the National Society for the Study of Education*, 27(1): 219–316.

Burt, C. 1955. The evidence for the concept of intelligence. *British Journal of Educational Psychology*, 25(3): 158–77.

—— 1958. The inheritance of mental ability. *American Psychologist*, 13: 1–15.

—— 1966. The genetic determination of differences in intelligence: A study of monozygotic twins reared together and apart. *British Journal of Psychology*, 57: 137–53.

Buss, D. 1995. Psychological sex differences: Origins through sexual selection. American *Psychologist*, 50: 164–8.

Campbell, F. A., Helms, R., Sparling, J. J. & Ramey, C. T. 1998. Early-childhood programs and success in school: The Abecedarian Study. In W. S. Barnett & S. S. Boocock, eds., *Early care and education for children in poverty: Promises, programs, and long-term results*, pp. 145–66. Albany, NY: State University of New York Press.

Campione, J. C. & Brown, A. L. 1978. Toward a theory of intelligence: Contributions from research with retarded children. *Intelligence*, 2: 279–304.

Campione, J. C., Brown, A. L. & Ferrara, R. A. 1982. Mental retardation and intelligence. In R. J. Sternberg, ed., *Handbook of human intelligence*, pp. 392–490. New York: Cambridge University Press.

Carroll, J. B. 1982. The measurement of intelligence. In R. J. Sternberg, ed., *Handbook of human intelligence*, pp. 29–120. New York: Cambridge University Press.

—— 1993. *Human cognitive abilities: A survey of factor-analytic studies*, pp. 631–55. New York: Cambridge University Press.

Case, R. 1985. *Intellectual development: Birth to adulthood*. New York: Academic Press.

—— 1999. Conceptual development. In M. Bennett, ed., *Developmental psychology: Achievements and prospects*, pp. 36–54. New York: Psychology Press.

Cattell, J. M. 1890. Mental tests and measurements. *Mind*, 15: 373–80.

Cattell, R. B. & Cattell, A. K. S. 1963. *Test of g: Culture Fair, Scale 3*. Champaign, IL: Institute for Personality and Ability Testing.

Ceci, S. J. 1996. *On Intelligence: A Bioecological Treatise on Intellectual Development*. Cambridge, MA: Harvard University Press.

Ceci, S. J. & Roazzi, A. 1994. The effects of context on cognition: Postcards from Brazil. In R. J. Sternberg & R. K. Wagner, eds., *Mind in context: Interactionist perspectives on human intelligence*, pp. 74–101. New York: Cambridge University Press.

Chen, J. Q., ed. 1998. *Project Zero frameworks for early childhood education, Volume 2. Project Spectrum: Early learning activities*. New York: Teachers College Press.

Chen, J. Q., Krechevsky, M., Viens, J. & Isberg, E., eds.. 1998. *Project Zero frameworks for early childhood education, Volume 1. Building on children's strengths: The experience of Project Spectrum*. New York: Teachers College Press.

Christoff, K. & Gabrieli, J. D. E. 2000. The frontopolar cortex and human cognition: Evidence for a rostrocaudal hierarchical organization within the human prefrontal cortex. *Psychobiology*, 28(2): 168–86.

Cianciolo, A. T. & Grigorenko, E. L., Jarvin, L., Gil, G., Drebot, M. & Sternberg, R. J., n.d.. Tacit knowledge and practical intelligence: Advancements in measurement and construct validity. Unpublished.

Collaer, M. L. & Hines, M. 1995. Human behavioral sex differences: A role for gonadal hormones during early development? *Psychological Bulletin*, 118(1): 55–107.

Daneman, M. & Carpenter, P. A. 1980. Individual differences in working memory and reading. *Journal of Verbal Learning and Verbal Behavior*, 19: 450–66.

Darwin, C. [1859] 1999. *The origin of species*. New York: Bantam Books.

Das, J. P. 1994 Eastern views of intelligence. In R. J. Sternberg, ed., *Encyclopedia of human intelligence*, pp. 387–91. New York: Macmillan.

Das, J. P., Kirby, J. R. & Jarman, R. F. 1979. *Simultaneous and successive cognitive processes*. New York: Academic Press.

Das, J. P., Naglieri, J. A. & Kirby, J. R. 1994. *Assessment of cognitive processes: The PASS theory of intelligence*. Needham Heights, MA: Allyn & Bacon.

Davidson, J. E. & Sternberg, R. J. 1984. The role of insight in intellectual giftedness. *Gifted Child Quarterly*, 28(2): 58–64.

Deary, I. J. 1999. Intelligence and visual and auditory information processing. In P. L. Ackerman, P. C. Kyllonen& R. D. Roberts, eds., *Learning and individual differences: Process, trait, and content determinants*, pp. 111–30. Mahwah, NJ: Lawrence Erlbaum Associates.

—— 2001. *Intelligence: A very short introduction*. Oxford, UK: Oxford University Press.

Deary, I. J. & Caryl, P. G. 1997. *Neuroscience and human intelligence differences. Trends in neurosciences*, 20: 365–71.

Deci, E. L., Schwartz, A. J., Sheinman, L. & Ryan, R. M. 1981. An instrument to assess adults' orientations toward control versus autonomy with children: Reflections on intrinsic motivation and perceived competence. *Journal of Educational Psychology*, 73(5): 642–50.

DeFries, J. C., Johnson, R. C. Kuse, A. R., McClearn, G. E., Polovina, J., Vandenberg, S. G. & Wilson, J. C. 1979. Familial resemblance for specific cognitive abilities. *Behavior Genetics*, 9: 23–43.

Detterman, D. K. 1982. Does "g" exist? *Intelligence*, 6: 99–108.

Dewey, J. 1933. *How we think: A restatement of the relation of reflective thinking to the educative process*. Boston, MA: Heath.

Dick, D. M. & Rose, R. J. 2002. Behavior genetics: What's new? What's next? *Current Directions in Psychological Science*, 11(2): 70–4.

Drasgow, F., Levine, M. V. & Zickar, M. J. 1996. Optimal identification of mismeasured individuals. *Applied Measurement in Education*, 9 (1): 47–64.

DuBois, P. H., 1970. *A history of psychological testing*. Boston, MA: Allyn & Bacon Inc.

Duncan, J., Seitz, R. J., Kolodny, J., Bor, D., Herzog, H., Ahmed, A., Newell, F. N. & Emslie, H. 2000. A neural basis for general intelligence. *Science*, 289: pp. 457–60.

Embretson, S. E. 1997. Measurement principles for the new generation of tests: A quiet revolution. In R. F. Dillon, ed., *Handbook on testing*, pp. 20–38. Westport, CT: Greenwood Press.

Engle, R. W., Kane, M. J. & Tuholski, S. W. 1999. Individual differences in working memory capacity and what they tell us about controlled attention, general fluid intelligence, and functions of the prefrontal cortex. In A. Miyake & P. Shah, eds., *Models of working memory: Mechanisms of active maintenance and executive control*, pp. 102–34. Cambridge: Cambridge University Press.

Engle, R. W., Tuholski, S. W., Laughlin, J. E. & Conway, A. R. A. 1999. Working memory, short-term memory and general fluid intelligence: A latent variable approach. *Journal of Experimental Psychology: General*, 128(3): 309–31.

Ennis, R. H. 1987. A taxonomy of critical thinking dispositions and abilities. In J. B. Baron & R. J. Sternberg, eds., *Teaching thinking skills: Theory and practice*, pp. 9–26. New York: W. H. Freeman.

Evans, G. W. 2004. The environment of childhood poverty. *American Psychologist*, 59(2): 77–92.

Feingold, A. 1988. Cognitive gender differences are disappearing. *American Psychologist*, 43(2): 95–103.

—— 1994. Gender differences in variability in intellectual abilities: A cross-cultural perspective. *Sex Roles*, 30(1/2): 81–92.

Feldman, D. H. 1980. *Beyond universals in cognitive development*. New York: Ablex Publishers.

—— 1998. How Spectrum began. In J. Q. Chen, M. Krechevsky, J. Viens & E. Isberg, eds., *Project Zero frameworks for early childhood education*,

Vol. 2. Building on children's strengths: The experience of Project Spectrum, pp. 1–17. New York: Teachers College Press.

Feuerstein, R. 1980. *Instrumental enrichment: An intervention program for cognitive modifiability*. Baltimore, MD: University Park.

Fiese, B. H. 2001. Family matters: A systems view of family effects on children's cognitive health. In R. J. Sternberg & E. L. Grigorenko, eds., *Environmental effects on cognitive abilities*, pp. 39–57. Mahwah, NJ: Lawrence Erlbaum Associates.

Fischer, K. W. 1980. A theory of cognitive development: The control and construction of hierarchies of skills. *Psychological Review*, 87: 477–531.

Fish, J. M. 2002. The myth of race. In J. M. Fish, ed., *Race and intelligence: Separating science from myth*, pp. 113–141. Mahwah, NJ: Lawrence Erlbaum Associates.

Flynn, J. R. 1987. Massive IQ gains in 14 nations: What IQ tests really measure. *Psychological Bulletin*, 101: 171–91.

—— 1991. *Asian–Americans: Achievement beyond IQ*. Hillsdale, NJ: Lawrence Erlbaum Associates.

Fuchs, T., Birbaumer, N., Lutzenberger, W., Gruzelier, J. H. & Kaiser, J. 2003. Neurofeedback treatment for attention-deficit/hyperactivity disorder in children: A comparison with methylphenidate. *Applied Psychophysiology & Biofeedback*, 28(1): 1–12.

Galton, F. 1869. *Hereditary Genius: An Inquiry into its Laws and Consequences*. London: Macmillan.

—— 1876. The history of twins as a criterion of the relative powers of nature and nurture. *Royal Anthropological Institute of Great Britain and Ireland Journal*, 6: 391–406.

—— 1883. *Inquiry into human faculty and its development*. London: Macmillan Press.

Garber, H. L. 1988. *The Milwaukee project: Preventing mental retardation in children at risk*. Washington, DC: American Association on Mental Retardation.

Gardner, H. 1983. *Frames of mind: The theory of multiple intelligences*. New York: Basic.

—— 1999a. *Intelligence reframed: Multiple intelligences for the 21st century*. New York: Basic.

—— 1999b. Multiple approaches to understanding. In C. M. Reigeluth, ed., *Instructional-design theories and models*, vol. 2, pp. 69–89. Mahwah, NJ: Lawrence Erlbaum Associates.

Garlick, D. 2002. Understanding the nature of the general factor of intelligence: The role of individual differences in neural plasticity as an explanatory mechanism. *Psychological Review*, 109: 116–36.

Gill, R. & Keats, D. M. 1980. Elements of intellectual competence: Judgments by Australian and Malay university students. *Journal of Cross-Cultural Psychology*, 11: 233–43.

Goddard, H. H. 1919. *Psychology of the normal and subnormal.* New York: Dodd, Mead & Co.

Gould, S. J. 1996. *The mismeasure of man,* rev. ed. New York: Norton & Co.

Greenfield, P. M. 1997. You can't take it with you: Why ability assessments don't cross cultures. *American Psychologist,* 52(10): 1115–24.

Grigorenko, E. L. 2000. Heritability and intelligence. In R. J. Sternberg, ed., *Handbook of intelligence,* pp. 53–91. New York: Cambridge University Press.

Grigorenko, E. L., Geissler, P. W., Prince, R., Okatcha, F., Nokes, C., Kenny, D. A., Bundy, D. A. & Sternberg, R. J. 2001. The organization of Luo conceptions of intelligence: A study of implicit theories in a Kenyan village. *International Journal of Behavioral Development,* 25(4): 367–78.

Grotzer, T. A. & Perkins, D. N., 2000. Teaching intelligence. In R. J. Sternberg, ed., *Handbook of intelligence,* pp. 492–515. New York: Cambridge University Press.

Guilford, J. P. 1956. The structure of intellect. *Psychological Bulletin,* 53, 267–93.

—— 1982. Cognitive psychology's ambiguities: Some suggested remedies. *Psychological Review,* 89, 48–59.

Gustafsson, J. 1984. A unifying model for the structure of intellectual abilities. *Intelligence,* 8: 179–203.

Guttman, L. 1954. A new approach to factor analysis: The radex. In P. F. Lazarsfeld, ed., *Mathematical thinking in the social sciences,* pp. 258–348. New York: Free Press.

Haggerty, M. E., Terman, L. M., Thorndike, G. M., Whipple, G. M. & Yerkes, R. M. 1923. *National intelligence tests.* Yonkers-on-Hudson, NY: World Book Co.

Haier, R. J. 2003. Brain imaging studies of intelligence: Individual differences and neurobiology. In R. J. Sternberg, J. Lautrey & T. I. Lubart, eds., *Models of intelligence: International perspectives.* Washington, DC: American Psychological Association.

Halford, G. S. 1999. The properties of representations used in higher cognitive processes: Developmental implications. In I. E Sigel, ed., *Development of mental representation: Theories and applications,* pp. 147–68. Hillsdale, NJ: Lawrence Erlbaum Associates.

Halpern, D. F. 1986. *Sex differences in cognitive abilities.* Hillsdale, NJ: Lawrence Erlbaum Associates.

—— 1997. Sex differences in intelligence: Implications for education. *American Psychologist,* 52(10): 1091–1102.

Halpern, D. F. & LaMay, M. L. 2000. The smarter sex: A critical review of sex differences in intelligence. *Educational Psychology Review,* 12(2): 229–46.

Hambrick, D. Z., Kane, M. J. & Engle, R. n.d. The role of working memory in higher-level cognition: Domain-specific vs. domain-general perspectives. In R. J. Sternberg & J. E. Pretz, eds., *Cognition and intelligence*. New York: Cambridge University Press. In press.

Harris, J. R. 1995. Where is the child's environment? A group socialization theory of development. *Psychological Review*, 102: 458–89.

Heath, S. B. 1983. *Ways with words*. New York: Cambridge University Press.

Hedges, L. V. & Nowell, A. 1995. Sex differences in mental test scores, variability, and numbers of high-scoring individuals. *Science*, 269: 41–5.

—— 1998. Black–white test score convergence since 1965. In C. Jencks & M. Phillips, eds., *The black–white test score gap*. Washington, DC: Brookings Institution.

Helms, J. E. 1997. The triple quandary of race, culture, and social class in standardized cognitive ability testing. In D. P. Flanagan, J. L. Genshaft & P. L. Harrison, eds., *Contemporary intellectual assessment: Theories, tests, and issues* pp. 517–32. New York: Guilford Press.

Herbert, B. 2003. "Breaking away." *The New York Times*, July 10.

Herrnstein, R. J. & Murray, C. 1994. *The bell curve: Intelligence and class structure in American life*. New York: Free Press.

Herrnstein, R. J., Nickerson, R. S., de Sánchez, M. & Swets, J. A. 1987. Teaching thinking skills. *American Psychologist*, 41(11): 1279–89.

Holzman, T. G., Glaser, R. & Pellegrino, J. W. 1976. Process training derived from a computer simulation theory. *Memory & Cognition*, 4(4): 349–56.

Horn, J. L. & Cattell, R. B. 1966. Refinement and test of the theory of fluid and crystallized general intelligences. *Journal of Educational Psychology*, 57: 253–70.

Horn, J. M., Loehlin, J. C. & Willerman, L. 1979. Intellectual resemblance among adoptive and biological relatives: The Texas Adoption Project. *Behavior Genetics*, 9: 177–207.

Humphreys, L. G. 1985. Race differences and the Spearman Hypothesis. *Intelligence*, 9: 275–83.

Humphreys, L. G. & Parsons, C. K. 1979. Piagetian tasks measure intelligence and intelligence tests assess cognitive development: A reanalysis. *Intelligence*, 3: 369–82.

Humphreys, L. G., Rich, S. A. & Davey, T. C. 1985. A Piagetian test of general intelligence. *Developmental Psychology*, 21(5): 872–7.

Hunt, J. M. 1961. *Intelligence and experience*. New York: Ronald Press Co.

Hunt, E., Frost, N & Lunneborg, C. 1973. Individual differences in cognition: A new approach to intelligence. In G. Bower, ed., *The psychology of learning and motivation: Advances in research and theory*, vol. 7, pp. 87–122. New York: Academic Press.

Innocenti, G. M., 1994. Some new trends in the study of the corpus callosum. *Behavioral & Brain Research*, 64: 1–8.

Jensen, A. R. 1969. How much can we boost IQ and scholastic achievement? *Harvard Educational Review*, 39(1): 1–123.

Jensen, A. R. 1980. *Bias in mental testing*. New York: Free Press.

—— 1982. The chronometry of intelligence. In R. J. Sternberg, ed., *Advances in the psychology of human intelligence*, vol. 1, pp. 255–310. Hillsdale, NJ: Lawrence Erlbaum Associates.

—— 1985. The nature of the black–white difference on various psychometric tests: Spearman's hypothesis. *Behavioral & Brain Sciences*, 8: 193–263.

—— n.d.. Mental chronometry and the unification of differential psychology. In R. J. Sternberg & J. E. Pretz, eds., *Cognition and intelligence*. New York: Cambridge University Press. In press.

Kamii, C. & DeVries, R. 1977. Piaget for early education. In M. C. Day & R. K. Parker, eds., *The preschool in action: Exploring early childhood programs*, pp. 365–420. Boston, MA: Allyn & Bacon.

Kaufman, A. S. & Kaufman, N. L. 1983. *Kaufman Assessment Battery for Children (K-ABC)*. Circle Pines, MN: American Guidance Service.

—— 1990. *Kaufman Brief Intelligence Test (K-BIT)*. Circle Pines, MN: American Guidance Service.

—— 1993. *Kaufman Adolescent and Adult Intelligence Test (KAIT)*. Circle Pines, MN: American Guidance Service.

Kirlik, A. n.d. Work in progress: Reinventing intelligence for an invented world. In R. J. Sternberg & D. Preiss, eds.), *Intelligence and technology*. Mahwah, NJ: Lawrence Erlbaum Associates. In press.

Krechevsky, M. & Gardner, H. 1990. The emergence and nurturance of multiple intelligences: The Project Spectrum approach. In J. A. Howe, ed., *Encouraging the development of exceptional skills and talents*, pp. 222–45. Leicester, UK: The British Psychological Society.

Kuhn, D. 1979. The application of Piaget's theory of cognitive development to education. *Harvard Educational Review*, 49(3): 340–60.

Kyllonen, P. C. 1993. Aptitude testing inspired by information processing: A test of the four-sources model. *The Journal of General Psychology*, 120(3): 375–405.

Kyllonen, P. C. & Christal, R. E. 1990. Reasoning ability is (little more than) working-memory capacity?! *Intelligence*, 14: 389–433.

Kyllonen, P. C., Lohman, D. F. & Snow, R. E. 1984. Effects of aptitudes, strategy training, and task facets on spatial task performance. *Journal of Educational Psychology*, 76(1): 130–45.

Laboratory of Comparative Human Cognition. 1982. In R. J. Sternberg, ed., *Handbook of human intelligence*, pp. 642–719. New York: Cambridge University Press.

Lavatelli, C. S. 1970. *Piaget's theory applied to an early childhood curriculum.* Boston, MA: American Science & Engineering.

Lawson, A. E. 1975. Developing formal thought through biology teaching. *The American Biology Teacher,* 37, 411–29.

Lawson, A. E., Blake, A. J. D. & Nordland, F. H. 1975. Training effects and generalization of the ability to control variables in high school biology students. *Science Education,* 59(3): 387–96.

Lazar, I. & Darlington, R. 1982. Lasting effects of early education: A report from the consortium for longitudinal studies. *Monographs of the Society for Research in Child Development,* 47(2–3), Serial No. 195.

Leahy, A. M. 1935. Nature–nurture and intelligence. *Genetic Psychological Monographs,* 17: 237–308.

Lewontin, R. C. 1970. Race and intelligence. *Bulletin of Atomic Scientists,* 26(3): 2–8.

Lipman, M. 1987. Some thoughts on the foundations of reflective education. In J. B. Baron & R. J. Sternberg, eds., *Teaching thinking skills: Theory and Practice,* pp. 151–61. New York: W. H. Freeman.

Lipman, M. 1993. Promoting better classroom thinking. *Educational Psychology,* 13: 291–304.

Loehlin, J. C., Gardner, L. & Spuhler, J. N. 1975. *Race differences in intelligence.* San Francisco, CA: Freeman.

Loehlin, J. C. 2000. Group differences in intelligence. In R. J. Sternberg, ed., *Handbook of intelligence,* pp. 176–93. New York: Cambridge University Press.

Lohman, D. F. 1987. Spatial abilities as traits, processes, and knowledge. In R. J. Sternberg, ed., *Advances in the psychology of human intelligence,* vol. 4, pp. 181–248. Hillsdale, N.J.: Erlbaum.

Lubar, J. F., Swartwood, M. O., Swartwood, J. N. & O'Donnell, P. H. 1995. Evaluation of the effectiveness of EEG neurofeedback training for ADHD in a clinical setting as measured by changes in T.O.V.A. scores, behavioral ratings, and WISC-R performance. *Biofeedback & Self-Regulation,* 20: 83–99.

Luria, A. R. 1973. *The working brain.* New York: Basic.

—— 1980. *Higher cortical functions in man (2nd ed).* New York: Basic.

Lutz, C. 1985. Ethnopsychology compared to what? Explaining behaviour and consciousness among the Ifaluk. In G. M. White & J. Kirkpatrick, eds., *Person, self, and experience: Exploring Pacific ethnopsychologies,* pp. 35–79. Berkeley, CA: University of California Press.

Lynn, R. 1991. Race differences in intelligence: A global perspective. *Mankind Quarterly,* 31: 255–96.

—— 1993. Oriental Americans: Their IQ, educational attainment, and socio-economic status. *Personality & Individual Differences,* 15: 237–42.

—— 1994. Sex differences in intelligence and brain size: A paradox resolved. *Personality & Individual Differences,* 17(2): 257–71.

Lytton, H. & Romney, D. M. 1991. Parents' differential socialization of boys and girls: A meta-analysis. *Psychological Bulletin*, 109: 267–96.

Mackintosh, N. J. 1995a. Twins and other kinship studies. In N. Mackintosh, ed., *Cyril Burt: Fraud or framed?* pp. 45–69. London: Oxford University Press.

—— ed. 1995b. *Cyril Burt: Fraud or framed?* London: Oxford University Press.

MacLullich, A. M. J., Ferguson, K. J., Deary, I. J., Seckl, J. R., Starr, J. M. & Wardlaw, J. M. 2002. Intracranial capacity and brain volumes are associated with cognition in healthy elderly men. *Neurology*, 59: 169–74.

Mandler, G. 2001. Apart from genetics: What makes monozygotic twins similar? *Journal of Mind & Behavior*, 22(2): 147–60.

Marshalek, B., Lohman, D. F. & Snow, R. E. 1983. The complexity continuum in the radex and hierarchical models of intelligence. *Intelligence*, 7: 107–27.

Mascolo, M. F. & Fischer, K. W. 1998. The development of self through the coordination of component systems. In M. D. Ferrari & R. J. Sternberg, eds., *Self-awareness: Its nature and development*, pp. 332–84. New York: Guilford Press.

McGue, M., Bouchard, Jr., T. J., Iacono, W. G. & Lykken, D. T. 1993. Behavior genetics of cognitive ability: A life-span perspective. In R. Plomin & G. E. McClearn, eds., *Nature, nurture, and psychology*, pp. 59–76. Washington, DC: American Psychological Association.

McGue, M. & Christensen, K. 2001. The heritability of cognitive functioning in very old adults: Evidence from Danish twins aged 75 years and older. *Psychology & Aging*, 16(2) 272–80.

—— 2002. The heritability of level and rate-of-change in cognitive functioning in Danish twins aged 70 years and older. *Experimental Aging Research*, 28: 435–51.

McShane, D. A. & Berry, J. W. 1988. Native North Americans: Indian and Inuit abilities. In S. H. Irvine & J. W. Berry, eds., *Human abilities in a cultural context*, pp. 385–426. New York: Cambridge University Press.

McShane, D. A. & Plas, J. M. 1984. The cognitive functioning of American Indian children: Moving from the WISC to the WISC-R. *School Psychology Review*, 13: 61–73.

Meeker, M. N. 1969. *The structure of intellect: Its interpretation and uses.* Columbus, OH: Charles E. Merrill Publishing.

Meeker, M. N. & Mestyanek, L. 1976. Can gifted children be taught to be more intelligent? *The Gifted Child Quarterly*, 20(2): 168–9.

Melnick, M. 1997. Methodological errors in the prediction of ability. *American Psychologist*, 52(1) 74–5.

Mendel, G. J. [1865] 1967. *Experiments in plant hybridisation.* Cambridge, MA: Harvard University Press.

Miele, F. 2002. *Intelligence, race, and genetics: Conversations with Arthur R. Jensen.* Cambridge, MA: Westview Press.

Naglieri, J. A. & Das, J. P. 1997. *Das–Naglieri Cognitive Assessment System.* Chicago: Riverside.

Nagoshi, C. T. & Johnson, R. C. 1987. Cognitive ability profiles of Caucasian vs. Japanese subjects in the Hawaii family study of cognition. *Personality & Individual Differences,* 8: 581–3.

Neubauer, A. C. & Fink, A. n.d.. Basic information processing and the psychophysiology of intelligence. In R. J. Sternberg & J. E. Pretz, eds., *Cognition and intelligence.* New York: Cambridge University Press. In press.

Neisser, U. N., Boodoo, G., Bouchard Jr., T. J., Boykin, A. W., Brody, N., Ceci, S. J., Halpern, D. F., Loehlin, J. C., Perloff, R., Sternberg, R. J. & Urbina, S. 1996. Intelligence: Knowns and unknowns. *American Psychologist,* 51(2): 77–101.

Newman, S. D. & Just, M. A. n.d.. The neural bases of intelligence: A perspective based on functional neuroimaging. In R. J. Sternberg & J. E. Pretz, eds., *Cognition and intelligence.* New York: Cambridge University Press. In press.

Nickerson, R. S. 1989. On improving thinking through instruction. *Review of Research in Education,* 15: 3–57.

Ogbu, J. U. 1986. The consequences of the American caste system. In U. Neisser, ed., *The school achievement of minority children: New perspectives,* pp. 19–56. Hillsdale, NJ: Lawrence Erlbaum Associates.

Ogbu, J. U. & Stern, P. 2001. Caste status and intellectual development. In R. J. Sternberg & E. L. Grigorenko, eds., *Environmental effects on cognitive abilities,* pp. 3–37. Mahwah, NJ: Lawrence Erlbaum Associates.

Okagaki, L. 2001. Parental beliefs, parenting style, and children's intellectual development. In E. L. Grigorenko & R. J. Sternberg, eds., *Family environment and intellectual functioning: A life-span perspective,* pp. 141–72. Mahwah, NJ: Lawrence Erlbaum Associates.

Okagaki, L. & Sternberg, R. J. 1993. Parental beliefs and children's school performance. *Child Development,* 64(1): 36–56.

Olson-Buchanan, J. B., Drasgow, F., Moberg, P. J., Mead, A. D., Patricia, A. K. & Donovan, M. A. 1998. Interactive Video Assessment of Conflict Resolution Skills. *Personnel Psychology,* 51(1): 1–18.

Pascual-Leone, J. 1979. Intelligence and experience: A neo-Piagetian approach. *Instructional Science,* 8: 301–67.

—— 1995. Learning and development as dialectical factors of cognitive growth. *Human Development,* 38: 338–48.

Paul, R. W. 1987. Dialogical thinking: Critical thought essential to the acquisition of rational knowledge and passions. In J. B. Baron & R. J. Sternberg, eds., *Teaching thinking skills: Theory and Practice,* pp. 127–48. New York: W. H. Freeman.

Petit, C. 1998. "No biological basis for race, scientists say: Distinctions prove to be skin deep." *The San Francisco Chronicle*, p.A1, February 23. Also available at http://www.sfgate.com/cgi-bin/article.cgi?file=/chronicle/archive/1998/02/23/MN94378.DTL

Piaget, J. 1970. Piaget's theory. In P. H. Mussen, ed., *Carmichael's manual of child psychology*, 3rd ed., pp. 703–32. New York: Wiley.

—— 1972. *The psychology of intelligence*. Totowa, NJ: Littlefield Adams.

Plomin, R. 1999. Genetics and general cognitive ability. *Nature*, 402, 25–9.

—— 2002. Individual differences research in the postgenomic era. *Personality & Individual Differences*, 33: 909–20.

Plomin, R., DeFries, J. C. & McClearn, G. E. 1990. *Behavior genetics: A primer*. New York: Freeman.

Poole, F. J. P. 1985. Coming into social being: cultural images of infants in Bimin–Kuskusmin folk psychology. In G. M. White & J. Kirkpatrick, eds., *Person, self, and experience: Exploring Pacific ethnopsychologies*, pp. 183–244. Berkeley, CA: University of California Press.

Poortinga, Y. H. & Van de Vijver, F. J. R. 2004. Culture and cognition: Performance differences and invariant structures. In R. J. Sternberg & E. L. Grigorenko, eds., *Culture and competence*. Washington, DC: American Psychological Association.

Prabhakaran, V., Narayanan, K., Zhao, Z. & Gabrieli, J. D. E. 2000. Integration of diverse information in working memory within the frontal lobe. *Nature Neuroscience*, 3(1): 85–90.

Prabhakaran, V., Rypma, B. & Gabrieli, J. D. E. 2001. Neural substrates of mathematical reasoning: A functional magnetic resonance imaging study of neocortical activation during performance of the necessary arithmetic operations test. *Neuropsychology*, 15(1): 115–27.

Ramey, C. T., Ramey, S. L. & Lanzi, R. G. 2001. Intelligence and experience. In R. J. Sternberg & E. L. Grigorenko, eds., *Environmental effects on cognitive abilities*, pp. 83–115. Mahwah, NJ: Lawrence Erlbaum Associates.

Rasey, H. W., Lubar, J. F., McIntyre, A., Zoffuto, A. C. & Abbott, P. L. 1996. EEG biofeedback for the enhancement of attentional processing in normal college students. *Journal of Neurotherapy*, 1: 15–21.

Raven, J. C. 1938. *Progressive matrices: A perceptual test of intelligence*. London: Lewis.

Ree, M. J. & Caretta, T. R. 2002. g2K. *Human Performance*, 15(1/2): 3–23.

Reeve, C. L., Milton, D. H. 2002 Asking the right questions about *g*. *Human Performance*, 15(1/2): 47–74.

Rende, R. D., Plomin, R. & Vandenberg, S. G. 1990. Who discovered the twin method? *Behavior Genetics*, 20(2): 277–85.

Reynolds, A. J., Mavrogenes, N. A., Bezruczko, N. & Hagemann, M. 1996. Cognitive and family-support mediators of preschool effectiveness: A confirmatory analysis. *Child Development*, 67: 1119–40.

Roid, G. 2003. *Stanford–Binet Intelligence Scales, 5th ed.* Itasca, IL: Riverside.

Roth, P. L., Bevier, C. A., Bobko, P., Switzer III, F. S. & Tyler, P. 2001. Ethnic group differences in cognitive ability in employment and educational settings: A meta-analysis. *Personnel Psychology*, 54: 297–330.

Rothrock, L. & Kirlik, A. 2003. Inferring rule-based strategies in dynamic judgment tasks: Toward a noncompensatory formulation of the lens model. *IEEE Transactions on Systems, Man, and Cybernetics – Part A: Systems and Humans*, 33(1): 58–72.

Rushton, J. P. & Jensen, A. R. n.d. Thirty years of research on race differences in cognitive ability. *Psychology, Public Policy, & Law*. In press.

Ruzgis P. & Grigorenko, E. L. 1994. Cultural meaning systems, intelligence, and personality. In R. J. Sternberg & P. Ruzgis, eds., *Personality and intelligence*, pp. 248–70. New York: Cambridge University Press.

Sackett, P., Schmitt, N., Ellingson, J. E. & Kabin, M. B. 2001. High-stakes testing in employment, credentialing, and higher education: Prospects in a post-affirmative-action world. *American Psychologist*, 56(4): 302–18.

Scardamalia, M., Bereiter, C. & Lamon, M. 1994. The CSILE Project: Trying to bring the classroom into world 3. In K. McGilly, ed., *Classroom lessons: Integrating cognitive theory and classroom practice*, pp. 201–28. Cambridge, MA: MIT Press.

Scarr, S. & Carter-Saltzman, L. 1982. Genetics and intelligence. In R. J. Sternberg, ed., *Handbook of human intelligence*, pp. 792–896. New York: Cambridge University Press.

Scarr, S. & McCartney, K. 1983. How people make their own environments: A theory of genotype-environment effects. *Child Development*, 54(2): 424–35.

Scarr, S. & Weinberg, R. A. 1976. IQ test performance of black children adopted by white families. *American Psychologist*, 31, 726–39.

—— 1978. Intellectual similarities within families of both adopted and biological children. *Intelligence*, 1(2): 170–91.

Scarr, S. & Yee, D. 1980 Heritability and educational policy: Genetic and environmental effects on IQ, aptitude and achievement. *Educational Psychologist*, 15(1): 1–22.

Seger, C. A., Poldrack, R. A., Prabhakaran, V., Zhao, Z., Glover, G. H. & Gabrieli, J. D. E. 2000. Hemispheric asymmetries and individual differences in visual concept learning as measured by functional MRI. *Neuropsychologia*, 38, 1316–24.

Serpell, R. 1974. Aspects of intelligence in a developing country. *African Social Research*, 17: 578–96.

—— 1982. Measures of perception, skills, and intelligence. In W. W. Hartup, ed., *Review of child development research*, vol 6, pp. 392–440. Chicago: University of Chicago Press.

—— 1993. *The significance of schooling: Life journeys in an African society.* New York: Cambridge University Press.

Sigel, I. E. 2002. The Psychological Distancing Model: A study of the socialization of cognition. *Culture & Psychology,* 8(2): 189–214.

Sigel, I. E. & Cocking, R. R. 1977. Cognition and communication: A dialectic paradigm for development. In M. Lewis & L. A. Rosenblum, eds., *Interaction, conversation, and the development of language,* pp. 207–26. New York: Wiley.

Sigel, I. E., Secrist, A. & Forman, G. 1973. Psycho-educational intervention beginning at age two: Reflections and outcomes. In J. C. Stanley, ed., *Compensatory education for children, ages two to eight: Recent studies of educational intervention,* pp. 25–62. Baltimore, MD: Johns Hopkins University.

Skodak, M. & Skeels, H. M. 1949. A final follow-up study of one hundred adopted children. *Journal of Genetic Psychology,* 75: 85–125.

Smedley, A. 2002. Science and the idea of race: A brief history. In J. M. Fish, ed., *Race and intelligence: Separating science from myth,* pp. 145–76. Mahwah, NJ: Lawrence Erlbaum Associates.

Spearman, C. 1923. *The nature of "intelligence" and the principles of cognition.* London: Macmillan.

—— 1927. *The abilities of man.* New York: Macmillan.

Steele, C. M. 1997. A threat in the air: How stereotypes shape intellectual identity and performance. *American Psychologist,* 52(6): 613–29.

Sternberg, R. J. 1977. *Intelligence, information processing, and analogical reasoning: The componential analysis of human abilities.* Hillsdale, NJ: Erlbaum.

—— 1987. Most vocabulary is learned from context. In M. G. McKeown & M. E. Curtis, eds., *The nature of vocabulary acquisition,* pp. 89–105. Hillsdale, NJ: Lawrence Erlbaum Associates.

—— 1988. *The triarchic mind: A new theory of human intelligence.* New York: Viking.

—— 1990. *Metaphors of mind: Conceptions of the nature of intelligence.* New York: Cambridge University Press.

—— 1991. Theory-based testing of intellectual abilities: Rationale for the Triarchic Abilities Test. In H. A. Rowe, ed., *Intelligence: Reconceptualization and measurement* pp. 183–202. Hillsdale, NJ: Lawrence Erlbaum Associates.

—— 1997. *Successful intelligence.* New York: Plume.

—— 1998. Abilities are forms of developing expertise. *Educational Researcher,* 27(3): 11–20.

—— 1999. The theory of successful intelligence. *Review of General Psychology,* 3: 292–316.

—— 2000. The holey grail of general intelligence. *Science,* 289: 399–401.

—— n.d. There are no public-policy implications: A reply to Rushton and Jensen. *Psychology, Public Policy, & Law*. In press.

Sternberg, R. J., Conway, B. E., Ketron, J. L. & Bernstein, M. 1981. People's conceptions of intelligence. *Journal of Personality & Social Psychology*, 41: 37–55.

Sternberg, R. J., Ferrari, M., Clinkenbeard, P. & Grigorenko, E. L. 1996. Identification, instruction, and assessment of gifted children: A construct validation of a triarchic model. Gifted *Child Quarterly*, 40(3), 129–37.

Sternberg, R. J. & Grigorenko, E. L. 1999. Myths in psychology and education regarding the gene-environment debate. *Teachers College Record*, 100(3): 536–53.

—— 2000. *Teaching for successful intelligence*. Arlington Heights, IL: Skylight Training and Publishing Inc.

—— 2002. *Dynamic testing: The nature and measurement of learning potential*. New York: Cambridge University Press.

Sternberg, R. J., Grigorenko, E. L. & Jarvin, L. 2001. Improving reading instruction: The triarchic model. *Educational Leadership*, 58(6): 48–52.

Sternberg, R. J., Ketron, J. L. & Powell, J. S. 1982. Componential approaches to the training of intelligent performance. In D. K. Detterman & R. J. Sternberg, eds., *How and how much can intelligence be increased?* Norwood, NJ: Ablex Publishing.

Sternberg, R. J., Nokes, K., Geissler, P. W., Prince, R., Okatcha, F., Bundy, D. A. & Grigorenko, E. L. 2001. The relationship between academic and practical intelligence: A case study in Kenya. *Intelligence*, 29, 401–18.

Sternberg, R. J. & Rainbow Project Collaborators n.d. Augmenting the SAT through assessments of analytical, practical, and creative skills. In W. J. Camara & E. W. Kimmel, eds., *Choosing Students: Higher Education Tools for the 21st Century*. Mahwah, NJ: Lawrence Erlbaum Associates.

Sternberg, R. J., Torff, B.& Grigorenko, E. L. 1998. Teaching triarchically improves school achievement. *Journal of Educational Psychology*, 90(3): 374–84.

Stevenson, H. W., Stigler, J. W., Lee, S. Y., Lucker, G. W., Kitamura, S. & Hsu, C. C. 1985. Cognitive performance and academic achievement of Japanese, Chinese, and American children. *Child Development*, 56: 718–34.

Swanson 1995a. Effects of dynamic testing on the classification of learning disabilities: The predictive and discriminant validity of the Swanson Cognitive Processing Test. *Journal of Psychoeducational Testing*, 1, 204–29.

—— 1995b. Using the cognitive processing test to assess ability: Development of a dynamic assessment measure. *School Psychology Review*, 24: 672–93.

Terman, L. M. 1916. *The measurement of intelligence*. Boston, MA: Houghton Mifflin.

—— 1920. *Group test of mental ability for grades 7–12*. Yonkers-on-Hudson, NY: World Book.

Thomson, G. H. 1939. *The factorial analysis of human ability*. London: University of London Press.

Thorndike, E. L. 1905. Measurement of twins. *Archives of Philosophy, Psychology, & Scientific Methods*, 1, 1–64.

Thurstone, L. L. 1938. *Primary mental abilities*. Chicago: University of Chicago Press.

Tishman, S., Jay, E. & Perkins, D. N. 1993. Teaching thinking dispositions: From transmission to enculturation. *Theory into Practice*, 32, 147–53.

Tracey, R. 2003. *SOI adds perceptual development*. Available on the World Wide Web at: http://www.newhorizons.org/strategies/styles/tracey.htm.

Tuddenham, R. D. 1969. A 'Piagetian' test of cognitive development. In W. B. Dockrell, ed., *On Intelligence: The Toronto Symposium on Intelligence*, pp. 49–70. London: Methuen & Co.

—— 1971. Theoretical regularities and individual idiosyncrasies. In D. R. Green, M. P. Ford & G. B. Flamer, eds., *Measurement and Piaget*, pp. 64–80. New York: McGraw-Hill.

Turner, M. L. & Engle, R. W. 1989. Is working memory capacity task dependent? *Journal of Memory & Language*, 28: 127–54.

U.S. Department of Health & Human Services 2003. *Head Start Program fact sheet: Fiscal year 2002*. Available on the World Wide Web at: http://www2.acf.dhhs.gov/programs/hsb/research/2003.htm.

Valett, R. E. 1978. *Developing cognitive abilities: Teaching children to think*. St. Louis, MO: C. V. Mosby.

Van Goozen, H. M., Cohen-Kettenis, P. T., Gooren, L. J. G., Frijda, N. H. & Van de Poll, N. E. 1995. Gender differences in behavior: Activating effects of cross-sex hormones. *Psychoneuroendocrinology*, 20(4): 343–63.

Vernon, P. A. 1993. Intelligence and neural efficiency. In D. K. Detterman, ed., *Individual differences and cognition* pp. 171–87. Norwood, NJ: Ablex.

Vernon, P. A. & Jensen, A. R. 1984. Individual and group differences in intelligence and speed of information processing. *Personality & Individual Differences*, 5(4): 411–23.

Vernon, P. A., Wickett, J. C., Bazana, P. G. & Stelmack, R. M. 2000. The neuropsychology and psychophysiology of human intelligence. In

R. J. Sternberg, ed., *Handbook of intelligence*, pp. 245–64. New York: Cambridge University Press.

Vygotsky, L. S. 1978. *Mind in society: The development of higher psychological processes*. Cambridge, MA: Harvard University Press.

Wagner, R. K. & Sternberg, R. J. 1984. Alternative conceptions of intelligence and their implications for education. *Review of Educational Research*, 54(2): 179–223.

Washington, V. 1987. *Project Head Start: Past, present, and future*. New York: Garland Publishing, Inc.

Washington, V. & Bailey, U. J. O. 1995. *Project Head Start: Models and strategies for the twenty-first century*. New York: Garland.

Wasik, B. H., Ramey, C. T., Bryant, D. M. & Sparling, J. J. 1990. A longitudinal study of two early intervention strategies: Project CARE. *Child Development*, 61(6): 1682–96.

Wechsler, D. 1939. *Measurement of adult intelligence*. Baltimore, MD: Williams & Wilkins.

—— 1997. *Wechsler Adult Intelligence Scale–Third Edition (WAIS-III)*. San Antonio, TX: The Psychological Corporation.

—— 2003. *Wechsler Intelligence Scale for Children–Fourth Edition (WISC-IV)*. San Antonio, TX: The Psychological Corporation.

—— 2002. *Wechsler Preschool and Primary Scale of Intelligence–Third Edition (WPPSI-III)*. San Antonio, TX: The Psychological Corporation.

Weikart, D. P. & Schweinhart, L. J. 1997. High/ Scope Perry Preschool Program. In G. W. Albee & T. P. Gullotta, eds., *Primary intervention works* pp. 146–66. Thousand Oaks, CA: Sage.

White, G. M. 1985. Premises and purposes in a Solomon Islands ethnopsychology. In G. M. White & J. Kirkpatrick, eds., *Person, self, and experience: Exploring Pacific ethnopsychologies*, pp. 328–66. Berkeley, CA: University of California Press.

Williams, W., Blythe, T., White, N., Li, J., Gardner, H. & Sternberg, R. J. 2002. Practical intelligence for school: Developing metacognitive sources of achievement in adolescence. *Developmental Review*, 22(2): 162–210.

Williams, W., Blythe, T., White, N., Li, J., Sternberg, R. J. & Gardner, H. 1996. *Practical intelligence for school handbook*. New York: Harper Collins.

Williams, W. M., Markle, F., Brigockas, M. & Sternberg, R. J. 2001. *Creative intelligence for school (CIFS): 21 lessons to enhance creativity in middle and high school students*. Needham Heights, MA: Allyn & Bacon.

Willis, S. L., Blieszner, R. & Baltes, P. B. 1981. Training research in aging: Modification of performance on the fluid ability of figural relations. *Journal of Educational Psychology*, 73: 41–50.

Wissler, C. 1901. The correlation of mental and physical tests. *Psychological Review, Monograph Supplement*, 3 (6).

Witelson, S. F. 1991. Neural sexual mosaicism: Sexual differentiation of the human temporo-parietal region for functional asymmetry. *Psychoneuroendocrinology*, 16: 131–53.

Woltz, D. J. 1988. An investigation of the role of working memory in procedural skill acquisition. *Journal of Experimental Psychology: General*, 117: (3), 319–31.

Woodcock, R. W., McGrew, K. S. & Mather, N. 2001. *Woodcock-Johnson III Tests of Cognitive Abilities*. Itasca, IL: Riverside Publishing.

Yang, S. & Sternberg, R. J. 1997. Conceptions of intelligence in ancient Chinese philosophy. *Journal of Theoretical and Philosophical Psychology*, 17: 101–19.

Yerkes, R. M. 1921. *Psychological Examining in the U.S. Army. Memoirs of the National Academy of Sciences*, vol. xv. Washington, DC: U.S. Government Printing Office.

Zigler, E. & Styfco, S., eds. 1993. *Head Start and beyond: A national plan for extended childhood intervention*. New Haven, CT: Yale University Press.

Index